Bad Can Be Broken

A Story of Cancer, Karma, and Courage

Raven White

BAD CAN BE BROKEN
A STORY OF CANCER, KARMA, AND COURAGE

THE HOLY BIBLE, NEW INTERNATIONAL VERSION®, NIV® Copyright © 1973, 1978, 1984, 2011 by Biblica, Inc.® Used by permission. All rights reserved worldwide.

iUniverse books may be ordered through booksellers or by contacting:

iUniverse LLC
1663 Liberty Drive
Bloomington, IN 47403
www.iuniverse.com
1-800-Authors (1-800-288-4677)

ISBN: 978-1-4917-4554-0 (sc)
ISBN: 978-1-4917-4553-3 (e)

Library of Congress Control Number: 2014916404

Printed in the United States of America.

iUniverse rev. date: 10/15/2014

Contents

Bad Can Be Broken is a memoir one won't easily forget, and its inspirational message is sure to encourage those suffering from addiction, abuse, or cancer. Readers will find a part of themselves or someone they love within these pages. It's a story they can take with them, not just because it's short but because it will dwell in their hearts long after the book is closed.

—Sandi Rog, international, award-winning author of *The Master's Wall, Yahshua's Bridge,* and *Walks Alone*

AHB—for teaching me true unconditional love at the tender age of seventeen and beyond.

KHB—for showing me amazing feats of ambition and optimism, and how to reach for the stars.

KMB—for constantly showering me with laughter, love, and affection. And for sharing your talent for beautiful art.

KAJH—my newest angel. I shall love, guide, and protect you as long as God's willing. You are perfect love.

MAS—for everything in the whole wide world. For loving me when I needed it most.

My love for you is indescribable.

Introduction

Before *Bad Can Be Broken* was ever a thought, I did not live a very healthy lifestyle. I drank heavily, at least six days a week, blacking out most of the time. I used meth occasionally, away from the eyes of my husband and family.

My life had come together so well just five years earlier when I met and married who I thought was the man of my dreams. Allen was so attentive to every part of me, except my drinking. He had no clue about the drugs, but the alcohol was enough to drive a wedge between us.

He knew that I had used meth in the past, but I had him believing I had quit. I didn't do it a lot. It was hard to come by most of the time, so when I did have it, I hoarded it. That's when things began to fall apart.

My mind was so distorted that I made myself believe my marriage was a burden. I liked to be free to do as I pleased. I didn't want a keeper to watch over how much or how long I drank. This became a problem. Allen wanted control of that, and I had serious issues with domination. Not only was my marriage cracking, but my insides were forming their own rebellion against me. I didn't know the fight I was about to have on my hands. A war was breaking out in my intestines, and casualties were possible.

The drugs and alcohol turned me into a liar, thief, and adulteress. Allen wasn't the kind of man to be treated the way I treated him. So on a cold December morning after Christmas, I left him. I got my selfish way and planned a divorce. But due to the relentless pain in my gut, which had persisted for the better part of twelve months, I was halted in my tracks.

Someone up above decided I would not live a carefree single life. And so begins my story of how stage 4 colon cancer would at first become my nemesis but ultimately become the reason I live a life filled with love, joy, and peace as I have never known.

Even though this book contains some very specific personal struggles, including being a cancer warrior, it also includes many of the challenges I faced long before accepting God and my diagnosis—trials I believe need to be shared. Every reader will be able to relate to at least one, if not more than one, matter of adversity strung throughout my life's story.

Each chapter deals with different events I had to face such as abuse, death, and addiction. Every person has experienced or knows someone who has experienced some of the same obstacles I have survived.

This is not a cancer memoir. It offers hope and inspiration in some of the darkest areas we all face. It touches on spirituality as well as maturing as a human being. That is what makes this book unique. It is my original spin on a wealth of information about what happens in life and how much better we can become if we use our experiences as lessons.

If there's one thing I hope you take away from my description of surviving, it is this: never give up. There's a reason you're on this earth. No matter what you've been through or are going through right now, if you're just lost and need some direction, this book will help you focus on the purpose you are seeking.

My message from God about why I must share my story was clear: "To give light to those who sit in darkness and the shadow of death" (Luke 1:79 NKJV).

At the end of each chapter you will find the "Recap" section. These are things I've listed about the chapter that I believe may help you understand the finer points of the material.

Part 1

CANCER

Though you have made me see troubles, many and bitter, you will restore my life again; from the depths of the earth you will again bring me up. You will increase my honor and comfort me once more.

Psalm 71:20–21 NIV

Chapter One

GOD'S MEGAPHONE

When facing a death sentence, you either speak to God or He speaks to you.

I will never forget His words: "I have given you a good life, Raven. Why are you forsaking it?" The message was precise. I had no idea the sensational meaning it would carry in just a matter of six months.

Thirty-nine years old, with three grown children, I was contemplating another divorce. I had left my husband and our marital home to live the life of a gypsy gone wild. My resistance stemmed from years of being controlled and hating being told what to do. I believed in freedom of the heart, mind, and soul. I was not a cat without claws to be kept indoors. Feeling captive made me want to shred my way out through the screen. Rebellious and willful, I never let anything get in the way of my appetite for fun. I hated rules and restrictions. On my own at fourteen, my body became a cauldron to countless poisons. I spent years stewing my organs in lethal concoctions of alcohol, meth, marijuana, and cocaine, not to mention the hours spent nursing hundreds of cigarette headaches and hangovers.

Running from relationships and self-medicating became routine.

After only three years, my second marriage had become bland. I decided that I no longer wanted the dismal constrictions of daily life as a couple. I wanted adventure, excitement, and the pleasures of mischief. I was bored and wanted out—out to drink myself into oblivion, bed down with another man, and devour dope without backlash and confrontation from a man who had never tried drugs and didn't understand the lure of them.

Allen was easygoing, charming, and sensitive, but he was fed up with me as well. He liked to drink and socialize, but the more we did, the more intolerable I became—"a different person," he would say. My behavior had caused the breakdown of our union. Not caring, I retreated to my self-indulgent nature, hoping to forget all about him.

Two days after Christmas 2011, I packed a few bags and rented a room above the bar where I worked, convenient for the seething alcoholic I'd become. It didn't take long to settle in and begin my double-vision way of living. I was high and once again the boss of my own ruin. Little did I know that in just a couple of months, I would be drop-kicked back to the home I had proclaimed was so dull and monotonous. Everything happens for a reason, and God would make sure I listened and understood why.

On February 1, 2012, during my self-absorbed hiatus, I woke up with a vodka-saturated liver and a relentless cramping in my stomach. Built with a small but muscular frame, I was known for being able to hold my liquor and lots of it. At 120 pounds, I never got sick, no matter how much I drank or how many different flavors I added to the mix. My stomach discomfort had been going on for months—over a year, to be exact. The cramps felt similar to labor pains and a demanding need to poop, although most of the time hardly anything would evacuate. I ignored it, telling myself it was just constipation, premenopause, something I had done, hunger, or the result of drinking too much the night before. I kept making excuses—for everything. I was good at that. But on this day, ibuprofen wouldn't cut through the pain. As a last resort, I called my estranged husband to drive me to the ER. He knew about this problem and had encouraged me to see a doctor, but I had always refused.

My mother and oldest daughter arrived a little later, and we all sat silently in the hospital room, waiting anxiously for the doctor's return with the results that would hopefully give us a diagnosis from the CAT scan.

He entered the room and began his explanation of what had been causing the agonizing misery in my abdomen for the past year. "According to the CAT scan, you seem to have a mass in your ovaries. Most of these types of tumors are easily removed with surgery, and the cancer doesn't—"

"Wait. What? Back up a minute." I waved my hand as if waving away his words. "But it's not cancer?"

"Yes, I'm afraid that's what it looks like."

Shocked and disoriented, I sat staring at him in disbelief. Tears began to fall. My mother rubbed my leg, and my husband reached for my hand.

"You're going to need a biopsy. We'll set you up with a gynecological oncologist as soon as we can." His words trailed off.

I was already somewhere else in my thoughts—there, but not there. After months and months of dealing with cramps, constipation, and irregular bowel movements and completely denying it was anything serious, I had *cancer*! No one ever wants to hear it. Yet, seventeen days before my fortieth birthday, I would. The road that lay ahead would be one of confusion, shock, sickness, sadness, and denial, just a pit of mental and physical chaos. Would lucidity ever be within my reach? I was doubtful.

Why was this happening? I couldn't believe *this* was real. My daughter looked terrified, but I could tell she was trying to be strong. She never liked to show her emotions or cry in front of anyone, traits she had inherited from me. All I managed to speak through my sobs was telling my daughter to call my other children. My husband held my hand and said, "It's gonna be okay. We'll get through it." That wasn't very comforting. We weren't even together. I was still in selfish mode. My stubbornness to be single was rooted deeper than a hundred-year-old oak. It was all too much to contemplate at the moment.

"*It can't be,*" I kept telling myself. It's benign. I was sure of it. I'm too young. I have three grown children. This was supposed to be the beginning of a new life. With the kids gone, it was my time, my time to start enjoying and living life like I wanted—no worries, no boundaries, no one to control me. I was about to turn forty and turn over a new leaf—well, actually an old one—and get back to the real me, the cool chick who did what she wanted when she wanted. I had made up my mind. I was going to live my life how I chose. The diagnosis was just another hindrance and hurdle I had to climb over. I was certainly used to those.

We'd all had a long night. They had no reason to stay, and it was late. Allen, my mom, and my daughter were hugging me good-bye, the three of them offering me reassurance. I was kept at the hospital for observation, and after everyone left, the tears rolled out again. I pulled out my secret phone and dialed my covert lover. I had to tell him about the cancer situation. We talked and cried for a while. I wasn't ready to tell him it was over. Besides, it wasn't that serious, and I would be back before he could say "Rumplestiltskin."

Scared and alone, I cried most of the night. Isolated with my thoughts, I remembered the premonition I'd had a few months before. I had been standing in my kitchen, bent over from the cramping and trying to mop the floor, while listening to the country music channel. Martina McBride's song "I'm Gonna Love You Through It" came on and stopped me ice cold. I watched, completely engulfed in the video, tears streaming down my face, and thought, *That's it … I think I have cancer.* The feeling was overwhelming and hit me with a certainty in my gut just as sure as the cancer that was there itself. My intuition overpowered me, and at that moment I knew. But I took a breath and, as with everything else, pushed the idea into the denial pit where so many other parts of my life had been hidden away.

Before leaving the hospital, I was coerced into going back home. In my mind, I was certain this whole mess would be determined to be bogus. It would be okay, wouldn't it? If I just kept looking ahead and didn't feel it, acknowledge it, or accept it, it wouldn't be so.

I told myself, *It's not that serious, right? As soon as I get this figured out and do what I have to, I'll go back to where I was. I'm not staying, and I'm still getting divorced. I might have to have surgery, but I'll get over that and be on my way.* Soon I'd be back to work at the bar, my illicit love affair, and my beloved vodka—the life I thought was so magnificent and grand.

About a week later, I was referred to an oncologist who dealt specifically with childbearing anatomy. "I'm not seeing a problem in your ovaries. Sometimes they're a little quick in assumptions, so I'm ordering my own scan and a biopsy."

Now we were getting somewhere, although this meant more waiting and worrying. Over a week later, the biopsy confirmed it was cancer, only the ovary was not the place of origin. The mass had developed in my colon not my ovary. No one knew why or how. It was large enough to look attached to both. From there, it was back to the hospital where I had started, to see a general surgeon for a colonoscopy. *This ought to be fun*, I thought. Actually, it wasn't that bad. I didn't feel a thing except the sting of the young, tall surgeon's words. As I came to from the anesthesia, he was just entering the room to release me. I looked at him in wonderment, and he simply said, "It doesn't look good. I'm going to refer you to a female oncologist who's recently moved here. She's very good and thorough. I'm also going to suggest you make an appointment for a Mediport insertion." I remembered a nurse telling me about those on that first night at the ER. "It's much better than all the poking and prodding, if it turns out that you need one." Looking back, I think they knew more that night than they were telling me. I believe they knew it was serious.

"So, what's my prognosis? Do you know what stage I'm in?" I asked, scared to hear the answer but prepared for it. He boldly replied, "Stage four," and walked out of the room—just like that. My husband told me later that the slender doctor had told him to pray for a miracle, that chances of survival were slim.

Stage 4? A Mediport? Cancer doctor? I knew from the minor research I had done between appointments that stage 4 was the worst, the last, and the final stage before death. In fact the statistics showed a three-to-five-year survival rate. This was not good, not good at all. My mind was so distorted at that point, I wasn't sure where I belonged, whom to turn to, or if (not to mention *how*) I would conquer this burden. My life was at a standstill.

I had seen several doctors by now, but all my information had come in bits and pieces. One: it looks like cancer. Two: you have a tumor—not in your ovaries but your colon—and it's malignant. Three: you have stage 4 colon cancer. By the time I saw the correct oncologist, I would get the unveiling and final truth. It would provoke every part of my disturbing past, hazy present, and shaky future. And so would begin my long and winding voyage into the devastating realm of being cancer's human host.

Nervous and still quite in shock, my husband, daughter, and I sat in the lobby of my new doctor's office. She was fairly young, and it seemed like I was possibly one of her very first patients. She was blonde, a very plain Jane, and wasted no time taking charge as her plan of attack spilled forth. She seemed a little nervous as well, dropping her files and pen and constantly wiping her nose. Maybe she wasn't feeling well? Still, she explained that my stage 4 cancer had metastasized to my liver and lung and had left subtle lesions scattered throughout my abdominal wall. Dumbfounded, I could not believe it had gone this far. I had let it get to that point. How could I have expected it not to after all the toxins I had unleashed on myself over the years? It was no wonder the disease was killing my insides after I had ignored it for so long. The doctor continued by discussing her goal for my treatment:

it would be palliative and not curative. That meant they would do their best to keep me well, but that was all they could do—ridding me of the cancer was not an option. No cure? No surgery? Nothing could be done but extended, indefinite chemotherapy infusions. With targeted therapy, as she called it, I could live years instead of months, as long as I tolerated the chemicals that would aggressively invade my bloodstream. "We want you to be able to maintain a good quality of life," she said.

Three thoughts constantly plagued my mind as she spoke: incurable cancer, how long, and quality of life. I was amazed at her ability to speak with such optimism as she was basically laying out the blueprint for my demise. When all was said and done, I would know the type of treatment (bearing the name Folfox/Bev), the starting date the following week, and all the dire side effects that could or could not be problematic.

At first I'd had no answers, and now it was all coming at me like a monsoon. I wasn't sure I was ready to rage against this storm, but I didn't really have a choice. Ingesting all that had been uncovered in the last month felt like swallowing a dagger. My head still reeling, my insides twisted and mangled, it would be some time before I could grab ahold of something or someone to stabilize myself.

In the midst of the grim prognosis, I had once again packed my stuff and hauled it back home. It was my only option since I was in no shape emotionally or physically to make any more decisions. I remained adamant in my self-centered, egocentric, careless mind that I was not staying. I would get divorced and continue down my path of destruction and splendidly sinful revels, no matter whom or what it cost me. Brainwashing myself into believing that I was eventually going to be independent again, I was eager to dilute myself in Jäger bombs and butter crowns, making all the world right again. I was in such denial. I truly believed that after a little treatment it would become nothing but a ghost in my patient file.

But God had made very different arrangements. The kids, Allen, and the rest of my family were pretending as if nothing had changed, nothing had happened as far as my marital relationship, and somehow this whole cancer snag had set everything right, made it better, and saved the previous life we'd all had. Selfishly, stubbornly kicking and screaming in my mind, I knew they were right. Home was where I should be. But I was not yet ready to admit it. I hid in the laundry room and dialed the secret phone one last time. This time I had to tell him I was ending it. And there was just no way he could endure what I was about to go through. I had to set him free.

Cancer might have infringed on my recreational activities, but like every other time in my life, I could just walk away and live as if there were no consequences. Ha! I was in for a rude awakening—literally. My denial would be set straight. My days of running would be no more. My days of being a drug- and alcohol-induced seductive tramp—over. I thought the karma-infested disease called cancer was punishment enough, but it wouldn't end there. Another stunning discovery was around the bend. And that bend would just about break me. As if my diagnosis hadn't walloped me upside the head enough, this next unexpected occurrence would throw me into a whole new, even more distressing reality. It would change the essence of my womanhood, my outlook, and my social life in their entirety—forever.

One month into my chemotherapy, the side effects were rearing their ugly heads. I suffered through nausea, vomiting, and pain so debilitating I had to take oxycodone every six hours with Dilaudid and Norco in between. I could barely eat or drink. I sweat profusely. I must have lain in bed for two weeks, until finally one evening, the pain was so unbearable I thought I was dying. My husband called my mother, a certified nurse's assistant at a nearby rest home. He conveyed how strong my pain was and that I was unable to move. "Call an ambulance," was all she said. I was certainly hoping the EMTs had something stronger than the meds I had, or I'd never make the forty-five-minute drive.

They got me loaded as I cringed and moaned. "On a scale of one to ten, how bad is your pain?"

"Twenty," I said. The dose of Dilaudid they administered didn't even touch this torture.

"You have to breathe, Raven. It will help." I swore if that male EMT repeated that one more time … Between him and the female driver who brainlessly took the back roads, causing me to bounce and jerk, I wanted to strangle both of them.

"Hurry up," I kept moaning. "I need something more for pain." What was happening? What was causing all this excruciating pain, and why couldn't anyone control it? Finally, they rolled me into the ER and sedated me with morphine to calm me down and get me ready for an ultrasound.

I was feeling quite numb by the time the doctor tried to explain my horrible physical distress. Almost unconscious, I tried to make out his words. "You have a perforated colon and are going to need surgery, something we can't provide here. We need your permission to transport you to Bay Medical." A nod yes was all I could muster.

The next thing I remember is weaving in and out of consciousness in the hospital room. I saw faces and even talked to some of them, from what I'm told. When I was coherent enough to stay awake for more than ten seconds, I saw my husband. He looked sad and worried. I thought I'd be opened up, sewed up, and on my way. But the devastating reality was dangling right there, left of my belly button. I had a colostomy bag. A bag to hold shit. A bag to hold shit attached to *my body*. I think I passed out again. After staring at it for days, I really felt my life was over. I was crushed. All the devastation I had sustained in the last couple months, and now I was stuck with a colostomy bag? I was a fairly young, vibrant, energized woman with a zest for social living, and it was over. It was all over, buried in a sea of prescribed chemicals. I was the recipient of a death sentence and now "fecally challenged" too.

The colostomy nurse visited me several times to show me how to clean and care for this thing, but I just couldn't. I didn't even want to look at it. The tears flowed every time I saw her. "I can't do this right now." I did my best to shun the stupid funky-looking thing. She was very sympathetic and patient. I, however, was in such a world of disbelief and sorrow that I didn't want to see anyone except my closest family. I couldn't fathom that this had happened. Wasn't a terminal illness enough? I mean, my life was never going to be the same as it had been, but now this too? I had been broken, my soul dismantled. Always having a plan, I wondered how I would get myself out of this calamity. For the next week and a half, all I did was push the morphine drip. I didn't care to think, feel, or see anything. My husband, who had been entirely supportive through all of this, had actually broken down. I had not seen it but was told by a friend. He had wanted to work things out all along and had fought against me leaving. Who could blame him for falling apart? His wife, who had tried to get rid of him, was probably going to die, and while waiting for that, she would have to carry around a bag full of dung. Unbelievable!

By the end of the second week I was determined to go home. I'd had all I could take from that place. I was ready to climb into my own bed and shut the rest of the world out. The protruding piece of intestine—that thing it made me sick just to look at—would keep me locked away for months.

My body was so thin and frail; 102 pounds was the least I had ever weighed. I couldn't eat or move for days. I was still in constant pain and weak from the surgery, and the laziness of the colon's new structure only produced more cramps. My days consisted of reclining on the couch, drinking hot tea, taking meds, and crying. Tears—and still more tears—of realization had finally hit me. I completely understood and started to accept the fact that my life would never, ever be the same again. No more going out with friends for a drink—no more going out, period. No more tanning in a suit on the beach. No more swimming at the lake or floating on the river. No more sex with anyone, ever. No more denial, just complete pain and depression for months. I didn't want company or compassion.

Unexpectedly, my husband, the angel I always knew he was, was the one giving me what I needed most: love, encouragement, and the words, "I'm here for whatever you need, however long it takes." I was starting to see a different man. The one I had fallen in love with and married. He was so patient, gentle, and caring. I'd seriously wanted to leave him? This beautiful soul who only wanted in this moment to take care of me? "That's my job," he would say. Things were starting to change. There was a long road ahead for healing, forgiveness, and truth; but through all the darkness I could see a faint glow, and in time it would be a flame rekindled, hearts mended, and a family brought back together by the grace of God.

My soul would take on its most healing transformation yet. *Hope* would actually become hope and not just a word. I began to pray again like I used to when I was a young girl, a girl who had been broken and damaged by those who took advantage of her vulnerability. God's invitation was there, and I accepted it. But long before I began God's work for the second time, the force generated by my abominable behavior had been cast to the wind and unfortunately got hung up on legions of unsuspecting and innocent souls.

Recap

If something is going on inside of your body that you're ignoring, my advice is this: do not put off getting it checked out. I had twelve long months to go get checked. Had I not been so stubborn and had I avoided making excuses, I would not be in the final stages of cancer.

Early detection can save your life. It can also help you to avoid all the emotional distress that comes along with a devastating diagnosis. And, trust me, sometimes that is worse than the disease itself.

Ask and it will be given to you.

Seek and you will find.

Knock and it will be opened to you.

(Matthew 7:7 NKJV)

C: collect your thoughts
A: answer to yourself and to God
N: never give up hope
C: call the people you love
E: erase your guilt
R: reflect and change

Raven

Part 2

KARMA

Chapter Two

DESERTED

My mother wasn't around much when I was little. She had a drinking problem and would leave me with a parade of relatives and babysitters. At one point, her younger sister and husband offered to adopt me. It was almost legit, but my mother backed out. She wanted to keep her baby girl, she would tell me later, not knowing that, by doing so, she would cause her baby girl to try to get as far away from her as possible. Her decision would alter the course of both our lives forever.

I was very aware of my surroundings by the age of three or four. I had watched my mother with a couple of different men and had witnessed her being beaten by one of them, which seemed like every night, though in reality it was probably only a few times. I can remember running across the field to the neighbors' house with my brother in the middle of the night to call my grandfather for help. Back at home the boyfriend was holding the phone hostage with a shotgun. I remember vividly the barrel of the long gun and my mother saying, "Let's get out of here before he shoots us."

We stood on the porch on an arctic winter's night, waiting for Grandpa. But it didn't matter. He was always gone by the time Gramps arrived. I still can't figure out why no one called the police—not Mom, Grandpa, or the neighbors. It just kept happening. Then one day, as my brother and I gorged ourselves on a jar of peanut butter, she walked in with a new guy. He wore a big brown cowboy hat, cowboy boots, and a flannel-type dress shirt. He was tall and skinny and had a beard that later reminded me of the country singer Don Williams. He was quiet but nice and seemed to genuinely care enough for my mother to offer her a better life.

They hadn't courted very long when, before I knew it, my mom, my brother, and I were packing up and moving to the city. Flint, Michigan, would be our new home and also where things started to get shady. But first, trust would be developed, and love would abound. It looked like a good life was in store for my older brother and me. But I would begin to realize as I came of age that a good life could truly be smoke and mirrors.

Our newly formed family was starting to fuse, but just as quickly, one of us would be gone. I was only six by this time, so I didn't pay much attention to this new man and his interactions with my mom and brother. I just knew that we were in a better place, a safer place, where Mom was actually home with us. She made breakfast for the first time that I remember, and the teacher didn't have to share her lunch with me anymore.

The new guy became trustworthy in my estimation due to the calm and comforting environment he was providing. By second grade, I had relaxed into my new surroundings. Stable and routine, it was home, the nicest we had ever lived in. By Christmas 1978, I had become quite fond of the new guy. There wasn't an abundance of gifts under the tree, but I was ecstatic about two particular items. The first was a pair of red, white, and blue street skates, and the second was a record player with a built-in organ, which I had never seen before and have never seen since. It was the seventies after all, and disco and roller-skating went hand in hand. I absolutely loved music, and now I had my very own machine on which to play the boxes of records in the new guy's collection. The albums consisted of Bob Dylan, Carly Simon, Elvis, and the Supremes, to name a few. When I wasn't playing those tunes, we would go to the local skating rink where I would hear The Bee Gees, songs from the *Grease* soundtrack, early Michael Jackson, and all the other great artists from that era.

Most girls played with dolls and Barbies at that age. Not me. I was content, savoring the sound of music. It was the one thing that occupied most of my time. My fondness for the new guy (whom I'll refer to as Newman from now on) was gaining points, and I started to feel like I had maybe, just maybe, finally found a dad.

While I was growing more affectionate toward Newman, my brother was not so enthralled. He and Newman didn't exactly hit it off. Newman would tease him, calling him chubby and fat and laughing at him. It was enough that my brother wanted to leave after a while. I walked into his room one day and saw him packing.

"What'chya doin'?" I asked.

"Movin' in with my dad."

And before I knew it, he was gone. He had moved in with his dad. He was my father too, but I wasn't acknowledged, due to my mother's promiscuity, along with his confession of love for her younger sister during their marriage. Our father was never interested in getting to know me, even though deep down he knew I was his. He couldn't deny my face. It was his face. But a daughter without a daddy conjures up a volcanic woman whose fiery lava slowly seeps out over time and eventually erupts until everything around her feels the burn.

I loved my big brother and was heartbroken over his departure. We had been through everything together. He had protected me and been my guardian when mom wasn't around. I guess my brother had felt snubbed and hurt by the harassment and annoyance Newman inflicted on him. It was a massive change, full of sorrow. All kinds of changes would start to unfold, none of which would be soothing as my little world with Mommy and "Daddy" would start to waver.

Shortly after my brother's ousting, I was informed that we were moving again—not just to another house but another state. Oklahoma was next on the list of Newman's plans. The dry, desolate state offered a bulk of work for the master electrician, and within a matter of days we were gone.

I was just entering the fourth grade at my new school when, during recess one day, my stomach ached so severely that I had to lay curled up on the bathroom floor in a fetal position. For weeks I would spend almost every day with my knees up to my chest, cringing until the cramping passed. Unbeknownst to me, I was going through puberty and about to start menstruating. I was so young and unworldly that I didn't know a thing about periods. My mother never offered up conversation, especially about private matters. In fact, she had stopped talking altogether—to me, anyway. She was distant and moody, and she rarely smiled. I didn't know it then, but I presume she was sad and mourning the forfeiture of her son. A thousand miles of misery kept her isolated at a time when I needed her.

During my adolescent change of life, I was lucky to have a wonderful teacher who discretely sympathized with her virgin pupil. My fifth-grade teacher, Ms. Retting, helped me with supplies and gave me one of the greatest and most beneficial books I have ever read, *Are You There God? It's Me, Margaret* by Judy Blume. It certainly resonated with me and was exactly what I needed. Ms. Retting must have known I had no clue and was scared to death. My body was reaching maturity, but mentally I was unprepared for the gushing red surprise. My mother never uttered a word. But thanks to Judy Blume, someone understood.

Our stay among the tumbling tumbleweeds in red-clay territory was short lived. We stayed almost two years until my mother just couldn't take it anymore. In 1983 we moved back to northern Michigan, the small town where my beloved grandparents resided and the place I have always called home. We moved in with them at first. The tiny two-bedroom home could barely accommodate five people and a dog. Mom and Newman took the spare room while I hunkered down on the couch bed. I had no complaints. These were the grandparents who had always taken care of me—the one's we'd called in the middle of the night for help, the one's I adored and who adored me. Looking back, though, I just can't conceive of how Newman stuck it out. He was sort of a recluse. He wasn't good at conversation, being shy and reserved and insecure. With no job, he kept himself closed off in that tiny bedroom, watching television and filling his face with nutty doughnuts. After a few months, we managed to rent a small two-bedroom cabin right across the street. It was filthy, but one thing my mother was good at was scrubbing a grimy house until it was spic and span.

With some urging from my grandmother we began attending church. She and my grandfather quit drinking shortly after we moved to Flint and became saved through the Assemblies of God church. It wasn't long before Mom, Newman, and I also gave ourselves to the Lord, and a very loyal religious routine ensued. And when I say "loyal," I mean strict.

It was almost fall, and I was about to commence sixth grade. School would eventually become a social outlet for me. I enjoyed church and the fellowship. School wasn't considered a place to socialize or have fun. My parents made sure of that. I was a true Christian girl in every sense of the word. My classmates nicknamed me "Sister Christian" after the Night Ranger song. I wouldn't know the song or band until a few years later.

I wholeheartedly believed in Jesus, God, and the Holy Spirit. I didn't notice then, but the policies and guidelines were outright ridiculous. It was unacceptable, *prohibited*, to listen to rock and roll; watch anything on TV that didn't have to do with God; associate with or have friends that weren't followers; use any profanity; miss any service; or disobey any authority—mainly God and your parents. I was expected to follow these rules to the letter, without question or falter. And I did. But not only those rules applied; my parents had a set of their own, which made life even more incarcerating. I would surely burn in hell if I were to sway from the gospel that I had been brainwashed into believing.

Satan was very real in our house. I was taught that he could possess you and cause you to live a corrupt life, ending with a toss into a fury of fire down below. If you were a sinner, you were going to hell. If you did anything other than abide by the law of God, the devil would surely snatch you up.

Now I believe my parents had somewhat good intentions, whether selfish or not. They thought they were doing the right things. I have learned, through my passage with cancer, exactly who and what God truly is, how my soul is connected to His Spirit, and that I am a part of Him. He loves all people whether they listen to rock and roll, country, or hip-hop. I realized that I am a magnificent part of God's creation, with a human border framing my soul. But those old beliefs were instilled, and I would soon reach a level of consciousness that would blow the rooftop off the whole sinister doctrine of our household.

By seventh grade, my friends were starting to question my parent's unwavering decisions and the control my faith had over me. "Why can't you go to anyone's birthday parties or school dances—or play sports or have friends over or trick-or-treat?" I was beginning to wonder myself. I kept asking for more freedom. "May I go to the party my friend is having?"

"NO."

"Can I play basketball next year? I really like it."

"NO."

"Do I have to return this box of chocolates a boy got me for Valentine's Day?"

"You will return them first thing in the morning."

I think that was the last straw. The humiliation of that one task started me thinking about what was really going on. I was a good kid, always on the honor roll, and I never got into any trouble. I was never rewarded for any of it. I never got to have any fun with my friends. I was not allowed to participate in anything outside of church, especially if boys were involved. It started to dawn on me why. All rules were initiated by Newman. I was not only his daughter but also something more along the lines of a possession to him. He forbid me to have any type of contact with other males. When my parents' friends visited and brought their kids, and they were male, he'd mope around afterward, giving me the silent treatment for days until I apologized for "disgusting" him.

"I'm disgusted" was the phrase he used when he was upset with me about something. I was made to feel guilty and disgraceful. I hated being made to feel that way, especially when I wasn't even sure what I had done. It would set me up for future relationships. It was from those occurrences that I would learn how to walk on eggshells around men, discover what intimidation meant, and become afraid to voice my opinion.

I was sick of being held prisoner for reasons that made no sense. I was starting to piece together all his idiosyncrasies: possessive, overprotective, controlling, selfish, and jealous. It was odd behavior since he was married to my mother, and some family members were making comments. Now I had an opportunity to change the way I was being treated.

Who, how, why, where, and when do not matter. The process of being truthful is difficult. It's what we're taught to do especially as Christians. Upon writing the specifics of this part of my life, I believe I received a message from God. "A talebearer reveals secrets, but he who is of a faithful spirit conceals a matter," Proverbs 11:13(NKJV) tells us. I have to believe He was communicating this to me to spare any wounds from being reopened. Forgiveness is the only way to heal, and it has taken years for all of us.

However, what I would like to disclose is this: when I was young, things happened to me that I didn't quite understand. Eventually, I came to know they were somehow wrong, but trust in the one particular person who was doing wrong made me very uneasy about speaking out. I didn't know how to go about sharing this information, so I looked up the word *molestation*. I had to be sure that I would state the correct term when revealing my fact. It means to touch or feel up, assault or abuse. And yes, I had the correct term.

My earliest memories of this mistreatment are from when I was four. Three different men, for whatever reason, felt they had the right to violate a small child. It happened once at the hands of each of them that I remember. The next and final, repulsive experience occurred around age eleven and ended at thirteen. The internal damage has haunted me emotionally and physically my whole life. When I was older, I had a difficult time letting men touch me sexually; it was so much easier when I was drunk. To this day I struggle still, even with my husband. The effects are deep and lifelong.

The man who approached me at eleven, knew how naïve and innocent I was. I wasn't scared. This man had gained my trust. I was eager to make him happy, so whatever he asked me to do to please him, I considered normal. For example, about once a month, he'd ask me to come into his room and undress at the foot of his bed. It was always dark with usually just the TV on. He'd stare at me for a few moments and make me do a circle, and then we were done. He had me believing he was charting my growth in some kind of notebook. Naturally, I didn't see anything wrong with it. I was so detached from the thought of anything harmful that I just went on my way happily skipping back to whatever I had been doing beforehand. There were other uncomfortable situations; but each time, I was made to feel "approved of," and the happier he was, the more he would spoil me.

After my revelation about the last man who violated me and put my mind in a place it never should've been, my mother and Newman decided to move back to Flint so he could go back to work. I moved in with my grandparents so I could stay in the same school and help take care of Grandma. My mother's leaving hurt immensely. I needed her encouragement and support to help me believe that everything would be all right. I would never receive it from her. I felt betrayed by her, but most of all, by God. Where was my saving grace, my Savior? If Jesus loved all the little children, where was this love? Where was my protection? I was accused of being a rebellious, defiant girl who wanted things *her* way. My mother never took the time to know me or to know my heart. When I became a mother, I may not have known everything about my children or been there all the time, but I made sure I asked them periodically if anyone had ever touched them inappropriately and insisted that, if anyone ever did, they tell me, no matter what. I was not about to let them encounter any of that kind of vile sickness from men who were obviously disturbed.

One thing I know for sure: when children come forth with stories about being abused, believe them!

In my mind, God had failed me. I started to doubt that He had ever been there at all. Maybe He didn't even exist. So I left Him, my faith, the church, and all the beliefs that went along with Him. After all, what had He done for me while I was faithfully on my knees praying, serving, and spreading His word at eleven years old? I was mad. I was hurt, and I wanted revenge against all of them. I realized later that He gave me the courage to speak up, but that didn't stop me from turning my back on Him then.

I was left with a deficient sense of self and belonging. It would become noticeable in my relationships with men and how I leaped from one to another without remorse, until I had put my children in the middle of it all. I would be on an endless search for love from men who didn't know how to love or how to handle my insubordination. Always feeling for the underdog or for souls I thought needed saving, I tried to give the love I so desperately needed myself. The love I had was in front of me all along; I was always carrying it with me but never letting it carry me. I was very juvenile but mature enough to handle most situations I got myself into, and there would be many. I was determined to get my fill of anything and everything I could get my hands on to cloud the pain, shame, and embarrassment.

Abandoned by God and my mother, and suffering the damage of being molested, I would try to deal with my trauma through drugs and alcohol. My poor grandparents didn't know what they were in for. I had a newfound freedom, and it was a bit overwhelming. I took off like a spooked whitetail deer, trampling anything in my path. The broken, the weak, the strong, and the healthy—I gave no consideration to any of them. God owed me an explanation, and my path of destruction wouldn't cease until I got one.

Recap

When you're a child, you don't think much about the future. You're busy trying to be a kid. Neglect and abuse are serious problems for our youth today.

If you have children, please stop and think about their needs and the things they say. If you don't have any, but you have nieces, nephews, or grandchildren, take some time out and spend quality moments with them. They will appreciate it more than you know.

Pay attention to their actions and the actions of the people around them. If you suspect anything shadowy, no matter how faint, talk to them. Question the children in your life. You may just save one from abuse.

Repay no one evil for evil.
Have regard for good things in the sight of all men.
Romans 12:17 NKJV

Dear Lord,
Please forgive my human nature.
May I be reminded of the spiritual good
in myself as well as others.

Amen

Raven

Chapter Three

BAD GIRL IN TOWN

According to Newman, the rule was always to keep my hair long and straight. The first thing I did was chop it all off. It was liberating and one of the first disloyal actions in a long line of future nonconformities. At fourteen, I was free of all the ludicrous boundaries fabricated and forced from the mind of Newman. I started making new friends. All the girls I had condemned before were now my guiding influences. They provided an image of contemporary life, introducing me to the latest music and trends in fashion, makeup, and hair. I was delighted by their eagerness to share what they knew.

Not long after, I began to notice that boys were noticing me—not just boys my age but older guys in high school too. I was cute, had a decent body, and liked—no—*loved* the attention. Attention—I would crave and love it from that time forward. I became a flirt and was considered a tease. My confidence was building along with the knowledge about how life was for youth, people my age. It felt good to be around people, different people, *sinning* people. By the end of eighth grade, I had met and started hanging out with Lana and Mindy, who would become my best friends and launch me into a whole new world of fun and all the things young girls should not do.

I had started smoking already, and as I walked home from school one day, a girl came running out of her house.

Racing toward me at full speed, she shouted, "Hey! Let me hit that cigarette!"

Lana was pretty, confident, and bold. She had a killer body with large breasts and a backside that wouldn't quit, and she topped it all off with a city-girl attitude. She had recently moved to town with her mother, a single parent, and had very little supervision. Her house was the perfect place to loaf around and get high without constant scrutiny. I loved being with my grandparents, but they were old and still involved in church. They were also blind to the direction in which I was being led. My grandfather ran loads of pallets in his semitruck at night, and Grandma took so much medication she didn't have a clue that I had been climbing out my bedroom window and not returning until just before dawn.

I was stimulated by all the diverse rubbish I was learning. I had dabbled in a little wine and low-grade pot, but the girls would show me the real deal. My new friends were way past that inferior stuff.

My job as a dishwasher provided the money we needed to purchase cheap cases of Old Milwaukee or Pabst Blue Ribbon beer and a joint here and there. They weren't afraid to take weed from their parents either. Every weekend was a party at Lana's house. I was having so much fun laughing, drinking, and getting high, I thought: *This is a great life. Who wouldn't want to feel this way all the time?*

Lana and I spent one Christmas break with her family in the city where she used to live. We snuck out and partied with a bunch of her friends. I ended up getting so obliterated on Everclear (liquor that is practically moonshine) that I fell out of a moving car and tore my hand up pretty bad. I didn't think much of it until I returned home to my grandparent's place. That night I woke to a high fever, an infected hole in my hand, and a red line halfway up my arm. I had blood poisoning. They took me to the ER only to hear that I would've been dead by morning had we not caught the vicious, life-threatening poison. This was the first of many times God would be watching over me.

I was positively captivated by rock and roll at the time, especially classic rock, the old stuff: Led Zeppelin, Pink Floyd, and AC/DC. I learned the artists and songs quickly. It was like my brain programmed every tune I fell in love with. I knew every word to every song and who sang it. My memory was excellent back then, even though I was killing it slowly. I knew all the old classic radio hits from before the whole religious recruit, but I had never heard heavy metal—and when I finally did, I loved it. It went hand in hand with every sip, shot, and hit, whether it be from a beer, joint, bong, bottle, acid or cocaine. The party was endless. Weekdays, weekends, it didn't matter anymore, and neither did school. I was all for getting and maintaining the highest high. Acid would become my favorite. The body buzz, the laughing, and the whole trippy process were incredible. I couldn't get enough.

I went from being an honor-roll student to a stoner in a matter of months. And I loved every minute of it. I finally succumbed to the fun-loving freedom I had and quit school altogether. I had better things to do. Getting high, getting drunk, and tripping on paper acid became my new goals. Far away were any thoughts of God or family. It was all about me. Whatever I desired, be it a guy, a drug, or a drink, I used my powers of seduction to get it. I had lots of male friends and sidekicks at my beck and call. This became a useful tool for me. I learned quite quickly how to use my fake charm to seduce people and get what I wanted. Manipulation was key, and I became very good at it.

At age fifteen, during a keg party, I met and partied with a married man, resulting in the end of his marriage. I knew his wife well. Not only had she been a babysitter of mine, she also worked at the restaurant where I was a dishwasher. I had never met her husband until that night, when he and another guy were competing to see which one would take me home. He won. She was out of town, and we both took advantage of it.

She returned home within a week and knew immediately. She tracked me down, telling me, "We need to talk." She took me to her house, where I had been in her bed just a week before. I walked in, not knowing what to expect, and without a word, she backhanded me twice. I stood there, not really in shock but because I knew I had to take what I had coming. She wanted to know all the details of my tryst with her husband. Feeling flushed, my face ablaze, I gave her the answers she wanted. I hated seeing the hurt in her eyes. Once she seemed satisfied, she dropped me off back in town, and I never saw her again.

I became the talk of the town, my reputation marred. Feeling scrutinized, rejected, and worn, I decided to leave town for a while. Things needed to blow over while I wreaked havoc somewhere else. Everything I did affected someone, usually more than one someone.

I left town with a gaping hole from the childhood abuse, my mother's desertion, my biological father's neglect, my new scarlet devil reputation, and the loss of the safety of God. Running, only to dig my grave a little more, I landed with my big brother and his wife, who graciously but reluctantly agreed to take me in. They approved as long as I consented to go back to school. Well, that worked out for a couple of months. Once again, I found an unsuitable crowd and indulged in my previous activities. It took no time to find like-minded brain-cell abolishers. There was only one problem: I wouldn't be going to high school. I had to repeat the eighth grade in the junior high building, away from everyone my age. I felt humiliated and ashamed—so much so that I stopped going and spent my days stealing liquor from my brother and sister-in-law's cabinet and getting annihilated. That didn't sit well, so I elected to get a job.

A bowling alley hired me to work at the snack bar. One chilly fall night I was approached by a confident, smiling man with a drink in his hand. He was nice looking and wearing a lot of gold jewelry. I had never seen a man in gold chains with rings on his hands. Guys in the small town I was from didn't wear jewelry at all except maybe a class ring. He began flirting with me, and I flirted back. He seemed knowledgeable, pleasant, charismatic, and older—much older. I believe he was thirty-six. Mind you, I was only sixteen, but I presented myself to be well above that age.

By the time I actually knew his age, we had already been on a date. Not a real date, though—we just hung out at his shared mobile home and got high. I thought perhaps this could be another way out. My mind started spinning possible scenarios. He was older and had a job, a car, and a place to live. He liked to party and wouldn't enforce any restrictions on me. He also had access to cocaine and weed. He could take care of me. Without a second thought, I packed what little I had, and off I went with a man over twice my age. I would soon realize what a mess I had gotten myself into.

I came to find out he didn't really have a job, due to back problems. The person he lived with kicked him out for not paying his share of the rent, so he ended up renting us a run-down mobile home in a seedy trailer park, with no furniture, no food, and just the absolute bare necessities. His car was on its last wheel, and I could see what a stupid idea this had turned out to be.

The end to this ruinous hookup came one night while we were having sex. We were in the position in which my virgin backside had never been stationed. Halfway through, the tears were streaming down my face. I had been transported back in time, reliving the horror of being abused by the older man who had molested me for two years when I was eleven. I was shaking and unable to explain why when he stopped to ask. He finally gave up and fell asleep, but I was wide awake, feeling sick at the whole warped situation. I had to find a way out.

The next day, I found a phone and called Lana, who lived two hours away. She enlisted a mutual friend of ours to come get me. Without notice, I bolted that afternoon. On my way back to the town where my reputation was skewed and I imagined everyone hated me, I decided to face it head on. I had few friends left, but it didn't matter. I was fleeing from the panic that had set in after my nightmarish decision. I needed my grandparents and their shelter. I needed protection and security from my ignorance. I needed home.

In the comfort of my small room, I started to release some of the tension between my shoulder blades, and the sickness in my belly began to subside. The adrenaline from having to escape the imaginary monster I'd shacked up with was starting to dissipate. The psychological impact reminded me that I was not yet a woman but just a girl out of touch with the very real and bizarre world. The memories of my molester came flooding in along with tears, taking me back to the first time. I had a lot of growing up to do, and it would only be a cycle of seasons before fate would have me on my knees, pleading with God for the first time since my mission of running wild had begun.

Recap

As a kid, especially as a teenager, I needed supervision. So many young people today are left unattended. We see the results of this in the news way too often. By taking just ten minutes a day to talk to your children, learning about their schedules, their friends, and especially their behavior, you might prevent the effects of peer pressure and combat some potentially dangerous curiosity.

But I will show you whom you should fear:
Fear Him who after He has killed, has power to cast into hell;
Yes, I say to you, fear Him.
Luke 12:5 NKJV

My coat is made up of many colors. A unique tapestry
of everyone I've ever encountered.

Raven

Chapter Four

MY RETURN

The initial shock of feeling trapped by a creepy older man was beginning to evaporate—that is, until I found out he was in town looking for me. An employee at the pizza arcade we hung at had given me that news. So I left a message for him. "I want nothing to do with you ever, so don't bother trying to find me." And so it was. I never saw him again.

I resumed full speed ahead into the enticing lure of the party world. Only this time it would include more drugs than booze. A male friend from high school, one of the few who hadn't shunned me, began hanging out with me more and more. We became very close. I considered him one of my best friends. He was easy to talk to and made me laugh constantly. He was smart, had a decent job, had nice cars, and always had the best weed and any other kind of drug we needed for a good time. I never thought of him as boyfriend material, but that's how it would end up. He was short and stocky and had baby-fine, straight hair and the cutest grin. I couldn't help but snicker every time he showed it.

I was never very interested in cocaine before, but he started showing up with a lot of it. That's when he (Avery) and I became exclusive. Our relationship was being built on mounds of white rocks. In our little world, it became a pandemic. It began increasing day by day until the days and nights ran together. I rarely stayed at home anymore. My time was wrapped up in the incessant need to have a straw inserted in my nose. Avery didn't play around. We snorted lines as long as the full-length mirror he chopped them on. I have no idea how either one of us didn't collapse from heart failure, given our relentless ingestion of the gasoline-scented powder. It wasn't child's play or insipid, low-grade snow. This was movie-star dust, good quality coke that made me feel energized, stimulated, sexually aroused, and able to talk about anything for hours. I was in love—in love with Avery for listening and for getting me high. He accepted me, understood me, and let me go on and on about my transient, troubled life.

We were inseparable at that point. I lost touch with most of my friends and family, stopping by my grandparents' house only briefly every now and again to give a quick hello. Hours turned into days, days into weeks, and weeks into months of nothing but cocaine brain. Finally, it was almost Christmas. We were sharing dope at a friend's house when suddenly I became very ill. It came on so fast I dropped the straw mid line and ran to the bathroom. Sour bile was the only thing coming up and out of my mouth. I couldn't recall the last time I'd had a meal; I lacked an appetite due to the drug. I hurled until my eyes watered and there was nothing left to throw up. I wiped my face, blew my nose, and went right back to finish my share. I felt fine until the next morning. The pukey feeling jolted me out of bed, and I spent the rest of that day hugging the toilet. *What the hell is going on? I must be doing too much.* I figured I should probably eat and put something other than beer into my routinely starved 115-pound body. I laid low for the next couple of days, but the barfing continued. I started to suspect something.

Sitting on the bathroom floor with my head in my hands, I thought, *Oh God. I'm pregnant.* That should've been the first thing I thought of—but oh, no. Lacking common sense, I had only that murky addictive fix on my mind until I could no longer deny the unavoidable. I was officially living with my friend, lover, and supplier by then. I'll never forget the shock on his face at hearing the news that I might be carrying his baby. Our drug-clouded days were now threatened—at least mine, anyway.

The doctor confirmed it a couple of weeks later. To my shock and dismay the precious little body growing inside me had been there four months already. I panicked. The thought of the atrocious amount of cocaine I had shoved up my nose was sickening—appalling—and I was scared to death. My poor baby was swimming in a bubble of Bud Light and bitter white poison, thanks to an irresponsible and senseless mother. Aghast at the notion that my newborn could come out deformed or mentally hindered, I immediately hit my knees and prayed like never before. My cocaine and alcohol crusade was done. I asked for God's forgiveness, but more importantly, I asked Him to spare the health of my baby and not let him or her suffer for my stupidity.

It would be a lengthy five months. I wasn't gaining much weight, not from the lack of eating but because I was skin and bones to begin with. By my third trimester, at seven months, I had finally started to show. At nine months, I looked like I had swallowed a basketball.

It was a hot and miserable summer. Swollen ankles, sleepless nights, and an ever-growing detachment from Avery made it stressful. But I was ready to meet the new love of my life. On August 14 my contractions started. I had no idea what I was about to go through, but I knew I deserved every bit of it. All I could think of was the story of Adam and Eve, how her defiance had caused every woman to have to bear the excruciating pain of such a blessing.

They call it hard labor for a reason. I spent at least twelve hours waiting to dilate and for the baby to get into position. I was induced at that point and spent another five hours in the worst pain I'd ever felt. Nothing was changing or moving, and my doctor finally realized the umbilical cord was wrapped around the baby's neck and he or she was too large to fit through my tiny birth canal. Preparation for a C-section was underway. At last, the spinal tap was injected, and I couldn't feel a thing from my neck down. After seventeen hours, a pudgy baby boy was drawn from my abdomen, assuring us all he had a good set of lungs. At eight pounds, eight ounces, he was perfect. Thank God, thank God, thank God. He had heard my prayers. He had shielded this exquisite little being that lay gently in my arms, staring up at me with big, sparkling blue eyes. He was flawless, and I was in love for the first real time in my life. I can't describe all the relief and joy I felt that day. All I knew was that I would give this little person all the love in the world and would never put him through such a terrorizing event ever again. At seventeen I had the greatest gift I'd ever been given. Now I had to figure out a way not to screw it up. But those nasty demons were circling me. They would try with all their might to pull me back down into their dark abyss. Would I follow or keep my promise to give my son his best life?

The answer would come four months later: a piece of aluminum foil and a toilet paper tube. A faster way to get high and more of a rush—I had to try it. Smoking cocaine, or "foils" as we called them, became the latest technique for us to find pleasure. I had fallen once again, thinking I could handle it all. We never did it around the baby, but it was lethal nonetheless.

"Come hit this." Those words would be repeated a thousand times over the next twenty years. The sound of the crinkly aluminum being torn off could be heard from every room in our tiny trailer. An eight-by-ten-inch piece of aluminum foil (sometimes bigger, sometimes smaller), a rock of cocaine about the size of a dime, and some water were all we needed to get a half-hour high. We'd mix the cocaine and water into a paste, spread it around on the foil, let it dry, and then use a lighter to heat the bottom to burn off any impurities. We used the toilet paper tube to inhale the smoke that rolled up after we lit the bottom a second time. To the taste buds it was like burnt marshmallows with an awful aftertaste. Since it didn't last as long as snorting a line, we were doing one foil right after another. If nothing else, it saved my nose from having a hole burned into it.

Almost every night we would lie down hoping for sleep, but as usual we'd toss and turn, heads and hearts pounding. Somehow, I kept my bearings, knowing my baby would need feeding and changing and a parent to console him and rock him back to sleep. He was a good baby. He hardly ever cried, and most of the time he simply ate and slept. I got lucky that he was not a colicky boy.

But perhaps if he had been, my cocaine career would've ended right there.

His father wasn't a lot of help with him, but he did go to work every day, even though he would make pit stops at home periodically to make a foil or a line. I believed myself to be a fit, attentive parent, taking care of my baby's every need, and I thought I was doing well. After all, he was a happy, healthy, bouncing baby boy. But the truth was, he had drug addicts for parents. As much as I tried to justify my behavior, I knew deep down that I was being a less-than-satisfactory mother.

We continued with our appetites for destruction, despite the responsibility and concern of being parents. It wasn't that I didn't love my child or care for his well-being. He was the light in my darkness, the only true love I'd ever known, and he loved me unconditionally for the lack of knowing better. He kept my heart beating and my blood flowing through my veins. I just thought I was good at doing both. I could handle it. I never got so completely wired that I couldn't maintain my duty. Except once.

It was the middle of the night. We were pretty hyped up. Uncharacteristically, my baby just would not go to sleep, and he cried every time I laid him down. My nerves finally caved, and I became so edgy and tense that we finally had to take him next door to Avery's sister. I was so ashamed and regretful that I swore it would never happen again. And it didn't.

My life was becoming mundane. I was growing weary and distant from the man whom I had so much adoration and love for; the chemicals were coming between us, and his personality was starting to change. He became possessive, demeaning, and verbally abusive. Everything I had confided in him, he now used to degrade me. The bond I thought we shared was resting on thin ice. Each day a new crack would form from his cruel intent. It was time for a break. But before I could build up enough courage to tell him, our damaged way of living would become nothing more than a pile of scattered ashes along the ground.

On a space cruise one day, high and alone in my thoughts, I was impressed with how Avery was able to hold a mirror, chop a line, and snort it—all while driving with one knee. He did the same with weed, nearly rolling with one hand. I was shaken back to reality as we drove into the small trailer court and up to where our tiny home was—or had been. Now it was nothing but a flat surface of blackened ash. Fire had devoured every last morsel of our belongings. All the brand-new baby stuff—gone. All our clothes and possessions, which were few—gone. I couldn't move. I couldn't get out of the car. Tears streamed down my face as the blur of words exchanged between Avery, neighbors, and family echoed meaninglessly. *What now? How? Why? Where will we go?* Gaining my composure, I slowly climbed out of the vehicle and walked over to the pile of wet, tarry ash. "Are you okay?" and "Sorry" stung my ears. Shaking, crying teardrops as big as ice cubes, I stood staring at the nothingness in front of me.

Out of the blue, someone came over to me holding a tiny gray kitten whose ear was slightly singed. I grabbed him and for a second felt a moment of gratitude. My eight-week-old kitten was alive and safe, and so were we; and that's what mattered. I named him Sparky.

I remember thinking that night as we settled in for bed at a family member's home, *This is a sign, a sign from God that things need to change.* What if the baby and I had been home and couldn't get out? But we weren't, and

I knew right then it was time for a transformation. We never found out how the fire started. It didn't matter. I had gotten the message. It hovered in my conscience for days. I believe God was saying, "You've lost material things. You are on the way to losing so much more if you continue this lifestyle."

I knew that meant my child or my life or both. I had to make a choice at this fork in the road. This was my chance to choose a different course. Would the impact turn me around? At the age of eighteen, I was facing some sketchy odds.

Recap

Babies having babies and relationships they're not ready for is another branch of the family tree that needs pruning. Do you have rebellious children? Do you know if they're sexually active? Would you ask?

If only someone had asked and cared enough about what might happen to me, a whole different life might have ensued.

Encouragement in studies, sports, outdoor activities, or whatever it takes to keep them occupied in the right areas could save your sanity and a life of potential problems for them.

Therefore I tell you, do not worry about your life, what you will eat or drink; or about your body, what you will wear. Is not life more important than food, and the body more important than clothes? Look at the birds of the air; they do not sow or reap or store away in barns, and yet your heavenly Father feeds them. Are you not much more valuable than they?

Matthew 6:25–26 Today's NIV

May the moon and stars hold you tight

And peaceful sleep be yours tonight.

May Heaven's angels keep your bed

And dreams of hope surround your head.

Raven

Chapter Five

CONFESSIONS

With the help of family and a few donations from local churches, we found a small but charming home just a mile away from our old one. It was midwinter already, and I figured my best bet was to hatch a plan and make my move in the spring. The thought of leaving Avery and raising my child without his father was distressing. My father had never been around for me, and I hated the thought of my little guy growing up that way too. But I concluded it was for the best. I needed healing. My mind and body needed a break from the drugs and from the mental anguish they and Avery had inflicted.

But there was no end in sight. The foils kept rolling out. My sensitive wounds were constantly sliced open by Avery's heartless, cold-blooded confrontations. By March I had found a job. With no driver's license (I had missed the training by quitting school) and with no interest in obtaining one due to my drug-induced stupor, I maneuvered the thirty-two-mile round trip as best I could. Nervous but determined, I glided into operating a motor vehicle with ease and comfort. Now I knew why all the kids who'd gotten their permits at fifteen had been so giddy. Driving was fun, and we looked cool.

By May my scheme was solidified. I grabbed the baby and my stuff and headed to my aunt's house, which wasn't far from my work but put enough miles between me, Avery, and the drugs.

The same aunt who had been intent on adopting me was now divorced with three kids and welcomed me and the money I would be pitching in to help with her plight. My escape from Avery resulted in a blowout between him and my protective grandfather. Grandpa had picked my son and me up after gathering stuff from my house. We had just pulled out onto the road when we looked back and saw a crazed driver barreling up behind us, nearly ramming the rear of our car. Avery wasn't just seeing red—it was pulsating through him. No one was going to take his son from him. I knew what was coming, but Grandpa pulled over and jumped out, cussing and waving his finger. Avery spewed a few words but backed off, and that was the end of our altercation.

He came looking for me once after that, but luckily, I was with some friends at a party and got away before he caught up to me. I was so done with confrontations. I just wanted to be left alone. My leaving must have sparked something within him to finally try and get on track. His parents got involved, and the next thing I knew, he was going off to boot camp. He had signed up for the army, which was way out of character in my opinion. But if it was going to help him, then I was all for it.

We bounced our son back and forth between us on weekends until it was time for him to depart. I still couldn't believe he was going through with it. But in a way, I was proud of him. I wasn't there for any good-byes, and it was just as well. We needed space from each other, time to heal, forget, and forgive. By that Christmas it would all be behind us.

Since the birth of my son, my mother had started trying to make amends with me. She was there all through the labor and had held my hand during the worst part of the pain. Every girl needs her mom at that time, and she showed up. We slowly began to connect again. I was young and virtually on my own with a child, and she desperately wanted to be a good grandmother to my son. I didn't deny her that, and I'm glad. She was a terrific grandmother, doting on his every need and being much more attentive to me. We strived to put the past behind us, but without us spearing the elephant that took up so much of the room, it was hard to breathe at times. I needed time to ponder the turmoil and madness decaying the parts of me that would have to be loved if I were to ever become functional and constructive instead of destructive. It would be a long, long road before we achieved anything remotely close to that.

We stayed with my aunt for the summer, but fall was creeping in. Her kids were returning to school and were no longer able to babysit, nor were they interested. Our novelty had worn off, and so had our welcome. With no money saved up, I had no other choice but to go to my mother's house in Flint. It was October. Newman would be gone hunting up north, so it would be just her, my one-year-old son, and me. It would give me a chance to recharge and rethink my possibilities. Mom worked, so for once, I actually got to spend quality time with my rapidly growing boy.

My favorite time was bedtime. We'd lie together on the pull-out bed in our room, and I'd read and read and read to him until he fell asleep against me, his little head full of sweat from the skin-to-skin contact. He was at peace and so was I. We had each other, and for the time being that's exactly what we needed.

As Christmas neared, Avery and I began exchanging phone calls. He missed us. Despite his previously mean exterior, I missed him too. I longed for a family for my boy and for me as well. I was never at peace with the separation, but it was necessary. During one of our phone calls, Avery confided how lonely and homesick he was. He wasn't sure he'd done the right thing in joining the army and couldn't stand taking orders. He wanted out, but how? And more than that, he wanted to get high. He asked me to send a joint via mail to the base where he was stationed. Still ignorant of the world around me, I had no idea this was a felony. I knew it wasn't right, but the consequences hadn't crossed my mind. Seldom did they. I did what he asked. A letter containing the dope was on its way. He would never receive it. Unbeknownst to me, all mail is examined for contraband.

A week later I got a phone call. Sergeant Michaels from Avery's base was on the other line. He said he needed to ask me some questions and that Avery was also listening in. I don't recall everything he said, but the one question I do remember was "Would you have sent this if he had not asked for it?"

My answer: "No."

It wasn't a long conversation, but I knew he was in trouble. I'm not exactly sure what they did to him for punishment, but about two weeks later I got another phone call, this time from his mother. "Avery's gone AWOL, and we're taking the motor home down to pick him up." I was surprised but not shocked. It was the type of thing he would do. He was never really good with orders. The war in the Persian Gulf was starting to kick up dust, and I'm pretty sure he wanted nothing to do with that, let alone having his parents worry that he might be sent.

By January he was back home with his mom and dad with a dishonorable discharge on his record. I figured enough time had passed that maybe we could make another go of it. I wanted my son to have both his parents, and despite all the hateful and hurtful things said between us, I believed in second chances. By the next month we were once again living together. His parents bought the house right next door to them, and we moved in. Life had turned around for a moment. No drugs—just me, the baby, Avery, and never-ending visits with his parents. I didn't know anyone in this new town, so my days were filled with coffee and conversation with Ma, trips to the post office with Ma, grocery shopping with Ma, bingo with Ma, and most nights dinner with Ma and Pa. It was fine for a while, but sometimes I just wanted my space. I've always enjoyed solitude and have never minded being alone, so the push, push, pushiness of his parents was getting on my nerves.

They started in on us about getting married, and that's all we heard, until we finally caved in and did it. It was either that, or Avery would have to start paying child support because I was on assistance and cheating the system by living with him. With no backbone of my own yet, I agreed to everything they presented, even though I knew deep down we were still on shaky ground and unsure about a real future together. I had no family around to consult with except by phone, and you guessed it, the only phone was at Ma's house.

Now I had a family but felt alone somehow. I felt overpowered by the three of them. I never had the courage to express my opinion. I hunkered down and did what I had to do to keep the peace. By July I was pregnant again. It was bittersweet in a way. Our relationship was teetering. The same malicious character began emerging from the man I was trying to make a life with once again. He was angry, resentful, and unhappy with our life, it seemed. We never talked anymore, so I never knew exactly why he felt the way he did. But he sure seemed to take pleasure in making me miserable. I was a whore and a tramp, a useless alcoholic like my mother. Those words hurt the most. I had strived to be anything but my mother. I was with my child; I wasn't out running around and leaving him with anyone I could. I was off drugs and alcohol. I was home every night making his dinner and taking care of our home. Where was all this coming from? Why did he hate me so much? I couldn't understand it, and I knew I was in for a lifetime of letdowns.

I couldn't live that way. I had no defense, no one to come to my rescue. With no family and no friends, I felt barricaded in that house, with prison guards next door watching my every move. They treated *my* son like he was *their* child. I was depressed, lonely, and caged. The only good thing was my healthy pregnancy. I held it together as best I could emotionally so the little life inside me wouldn't be upset too. But I knew she could feel the tension. Our nerves were tattered, but at least I didn't have to worry about a drug-addicted, abnormal, unhealthy child on the way.

On January 18, 1992, my precious, tiny, seven-pound, one-ounce little girl was delivered by C-section. This birth was so different than my first childbearing experience: a few contractions, some meds, a slice of the belly, and there she was, all pink and pretty. To hold and smell her was divine. God had blessed me with two healthy, beautiful children when I hadn't even deserved it. He had plans for me, I guess. I still wasn't ready to listen or even acknowledge that I needed to change my ways. I was on my own downtrodden path with a million wayward miles left to go.

There's something about having a new baby that brings hope and joy in the midst of a tumultuous relationship. It's like a new year, an opportunity to begin again and salvage what little romance may be left. It's all new and good at the start. But then slowly, day by day, the warmth starts to fade, and before you know it, you're right back where you started. A whole year went by with us trying to hold our little tribe together. I even got a job to help with support. It felt good to have some independence again, to be among other people and not just the in-laws, kids, and Avery.

I started to feel good about myself and the way I looked. I was out in the world again, but for me that meant trouble. I realized that I was being noticed at my new job. After I'd been beat down verbally, anyone's kind comments turned my head. It didn't take long for me to get to know the one noticing me. He was from Hawaii and had the smoothest, calmest tone I had ever heard. Sweet and charming, he wasn't like anyone I had dated before. He wore glasses, had thick, black hair, and was skinny but toned. He had something of a John Lennon look about him. By summer's end, I was having an affair. I could smile and be jovial with the family because I had something to look forward to. He made me feel special and pretty and wanted. I had that fever, the tickle in my belly and the heart palpitations that come with being infatuated with someone new. It was like a high for me. My days and pursuit were numbered, though.

Avery's mother began to detect the change in me and had no qualms about finding out what was going on. I guess I can't blame her. Her son was being taken for a fool, and she couldn't have that. She had a habit of checking and bringing me my mail. On this particular day, there was a large envelope that she just couldn't keep her hands from opening. She was a little nosy, but I never dreamed she would scour my mail. She pretended it was a mistake and that she thought it was hers. However it happened, the jig was up. The package was from my Hawaiian "friend," and the contents were quite spicy. She came squalling in, spewing profanity with every step. Stomping up to me, she swung her hand across my face. Stammering, her eyes full of fury, she looked me straight in the eye and said, "You're a tramp." Stunned, I took a step back and started to cry, my stomach gurgling with anxiety. I still had Avery to deal with, and who knew how the unsavory news would make him react. "Either you tell him, or I will." And out the door she went, still grumbling to herself.

The tickle from infatuation and lust was now knots of fear and uncertainty. He'd be home soon. I'd better figure out what I planned to say, and then, where I planned to stay.

Unsuspecting, Avery came through the door at five o'clock looking for dinner. Shaking and pacing, I waited for him to take a shower while I pretended to fix his food. Eating was the last thing I was thinking of. I got ready to launch my weapon of mass destruction as I followed him from the shower into our bedroom.

"We need to talk."

He sat on the bed, staring up at me with the engaging baby blues that I had once fallen in love with.

"I've been seeing someone at work."

Still staring intently, he looked at me as if I were joking. For whatever reason, he didn't fly off the handle, stomp around in a rage, call me names, or do any of the things I had expected. His pause lingered.

"Did you sleep with him?"

I couldn't look at him.

"Yes," I replied. That's when I began to fall apart. Despite the horrible way he'd been treating me and all the times I'd cried from a broken heart, I couldn't help but feel remorseful and sad. I hadn't had an affair to hurt him. I was just looking for everything I had been missing intimately, the things a woman needs from time to time: a kind word, a tender touch, a long, soft kiss. It wasn't the sex. I longed for love, someone to sincerely and deeply adore who I was on the inside as well as the outside. Avery and I had shared that once, briefly, but brutal words kill a person's spirit over time. And even though I had no hostility toward him, he had broken me. The love in our union had dissipated. I still cared about his well-being and state of mind, though, and the heartbreak I had no doubt inflicted.

Not much was said the rest of the evening. He walked over to his parent's for dinner, came back, and got ready for bed. As I was gathering bedding for the couch, he simply said, "I can't ask you to stay, but I'm not telling you to leave."

My body flooded with heat from my guilt. The lump in my throat was impossible to swallow. After all the repugnant words he had used to demean me, after I had admitted to being with another man to his face, he didn't want me to leave? I felt weak. Was it possible he still loved me? Could we make this work and move past each other's idiocies? I had a lot to think about. It was going to be a most unpleasant try for shut-eye.

Recap

Don't ever feel pressured to get married. When you marry young, you really have no idea what forever with one person means. You can save a lot of broken hearts by just waiting or by knowing for sure, without a doubt, that it is what you really want.

Divorce hurts more than just the people who were married. In my opinion, a law should require people to wait three years before tying the knot. That would give them time to really get to know each other (and hopefully themselves) enough to appreciate the kind of commitment marriage takes.

You have heard that it was said to those of old,
"You shall not commit adultery."
Matthew 5:27 NKJV

Become your own superstar before
glamming it up for anyone else.

Raven

Chapter Six

BROKEN HEARTS

In the days after my adultery confession I felt like I was standing in quicksand with no way to dig myself out with words or a shovel. I had made up my mind. I would be leaving again. I wasn't happy there; my feelings had faded, my heart hardened. To me, once you've been with another man, that's a good indicator that you're just not in love anymore.

My stubbornness and strong will had created a plan. I would take my children and head back up north. My grandparents were the only people I had. But they were aging, and I wasn't sure they'd be able to handle two small children in the house.

Revealing my plan to Avery would turn my world upside down and force a decision I will regret the rest of my life. I may have had a stubborn streak, but so did he. My proposal blew up in my face. With his parents backing him, I was warned that if I were to leave, I'd be leaving my son behind. They used threats of lawyers and court proceedings. How would I challenge that? I had no money. My family had no money. Easily intimidated,

I was up against a hard, cold wall. They wanted my son for selfish reasons. He was a miniature Avery. Three years old, he was an adorable, sweet, smart, handsome boy, the beat of my heart. I was his mother. How could they take him away from me? I was the one who cared for him, read to him, bathed him, fed him, changed him in the middle of the night, and took care of him when he was sick. Avery did none of those things. He wasn't equipped to be a single father. But he'd always had Mom and Dad bailing and saving him from whatever mess he'd get himself into, and this time was no different. I had no one.

Barely twenty and not yet ripe in my morals or my understanding of the meaning of marriage, I anguished over the thought of leaving my child. I knew two things: I was a good mom, and abuse never stops. I knew I couldn't stay. If I did, Avery would have even more bullets to fire, packed with paralyzing conviction. I made the decision to leave, promising myself somehow, someway I would get my son back.

On a warm summer's day, my mom and Newman pulled into the driveway. They would be my transportation back to where it all began. With my bags packed, and toting my one-year-old daughter, I reluctantly put her in the car seat. The tears began to fall as I turned to my precious little boy with the bright blue eyes he had inherited from both of us. I squeezed him as tight as I could for as long as I could. "Momma loves you with all her heart," I said. Choking back the tears, I did the hardest thing I'd ever had to do—let go. I tried telling myself it was for the best. After all, what did I have to offer him? I had no home, no stability, no money, and no job. As it was, I would have to depend on my grandparents to take care of me and my daughter on what little income they had. My tears fell like Niagara Falls as we pulled away, and I watched as his grandma took his hand and guided his little, short legs down the street to their home.

"I won't keep him from you. You can see him whenever you want." Those were Avery's last words to me. They were the same words I had said to him three years prior. I held my daughter's tiny hand, staring out the opposite window and weeping uncontrollably. Whitney Houston's ballad "I Will Always Love You," came softly through the speakers in the car. To this day, my heart aches whenever I think about that day or hear that song.

It was torture not having my son lying next to me and his baby sister. I couldn't rub his soft little blonde head or chunky, stubby feet. He would be starting school soon, and I would miss his first day. I wondered if he missed me or cried for me as I did for him. He was just a little boy, only three years old. I would lie there wondering if he sang his ABCs in the bathtub where I had taught him, or if anyone was reading to him at bedtime the way I had every night, and if he missed his baby sister. He had such a calm and loving nature, delicate and sweet, like most of my demeanor. Being my first and only boy, he has always been particularly special.

I have lived with regret and guilt over my decision for many years. In finding peace with God, I am only now able to forgive myself for foolishly believing I had no other choices. If only I knew then what I know now.

I did my best to stay in touch with him so he wouldn't forget me. I called at least once a week and sent cards and little stickers of monster trucks and baseballs. And true to his word, Avery allowed his parents to bring him up as often as they could, or I would drive the three and a half hours to see him or pick him up. It was hard; but we managed, and he didn't forget me.

Luckily, it only took me about a month to find a job and another couple months after that to get a place of my own, a small two-bedroom apartment just outside of town. It was clean, cozy, and empty. I had nothing to my name except my clothes and the baby's stuff. My brother brought me some used furniture: a bed, a dresser, and a small sofa. It was good enough and all we needed. Newman even allowed me to make payments on a car he had so I could get back and forth to work. They had moved back shortly after I did.

It didn't take me long to put to use my uncanny knack for getting what I wanted. The job I landed gave me confidence. I regained my independence. Feeling attractive and magnetic once again, I spotted a tall, slim, well-built young fella who looked mighty fine in his muscle shirt, jeans, and work boots. Usually a sucker for blond hair and blue eyes, this time I fell for tall and tan, with eyes the color of coffee. He was two years my junior, which made flirting with him even more irresistible. Those old, pleasurable sensations came creeping back around: the butterflies, the exultation of the chase. They overpowered my senses when I should have been listening to the voice saying, *You don't need a man or a relationship right now.* My divorce wasn't even final yet. It wouldn't be until August, and this was only March. I remember that spring well. The snow had just begun to melt, and the sun warmed the earth a little more each day. It made it easy to want to get out and socialize.

This frisky, adventurous, free-spirited twenty-one-year-old was ready to fang her way into freedom. Nothing ever stood in the way of my hunger. I wouldn't let it. That's probably why trouble perpetually followed. I didn't realize it then, but it sure makes sense now.

The young man—boy—enticing and tempting, lured me in with his good looks and the fact that he was off limits. He had a girlfriend. Burying my conscience under my selfish impulses, I went on the hunt. Empowered with my newfound boldness and defiance, I went in for the kill. So what if he had a girlfriend? I was older than both of them and worked at a pallet factory, which had turned my body into a sculpted, lean, muscular machine. I felt tough, fearless, self-assured. I had every intention of showing it all off. Using my playful, seductive persuasion, I toyed with him endlessly until I won. James and I were in bed in just under two weeks.

Bound by fierce sexual passion, our genitals were glued together every day for the next six months. From the bed, to the floor, to the roof, he had piqued and stimulated every nerve that had been dormant. The start to this relationship with James was completely based on pure sexual fantasy. But by August, the sweat-soaked sheets would begin to dry up.

My final divorce papers arrived, and I immediately felt ill. Dropping to my knees at the toilet, I began heaving my guts out, a nervous reaction to the delivery of the end with Avery, I suspected. I thought, *I should be celebrating, right?* On the contrary, the pit of my stomach was not doing somersaults of joy. It wouldn't be for the next several weeks.

I was pregnant. The pee stick confirmed it. Just my luck. I was finally divorced and working steadily, with a place to call my own where my kids and I could be together, and a playmate when I desired—and now baby number three.

I wasn't in love with James. I mean, it was comforting to have him around, and we were monogamous; but being newly divorced, it was not my intention to jump into another full-time commitment. With a wrench, in the form of a baby, thrown into my somewhat haphazard design of a life, I was inevitably, unknowingly about to embark on an eleven-year roller-coaster ride with no seat belt. This relationship definitely required one. At twenty-one, I wasn't even close to the yellow brick road of peace and serenity. And at times, my path would feel like hot coals beneath my feet. As I held fast to keep this new family together, life would become stormy, and hanging on would drive me back to the tornado of addictions that I thought I had left behind.

This roller-coaster situation would become one of highs and lows, with me riding with my hands in the air, waiting for the cart to come off the track completely and cause an end to all of it. I had so many close encounters, yet I'm still here. It really is a true testament of God working in my life. Without Him, I surely would be in an overthrown cart, lying helplessly in a pool of coagulated blood.

Recap

Here's a prime example of not getting to really know a person. Had we waited three years or more, James and I might have had a totally different relationship. Everyone has issues. Be sure you're ready to deal with every part of the person you're with.

He shall cover you with his feathers,
And under His wings you shall take refuge;
His truth shall be your shield and buckler.
Psalms 91:4 NKJV

Fresh air is the breath of God.

Raven

Chapter Seven

HEAVEN HELP ME

I had come to care for James throughout my pregnancy. Sweet and attentive, he was helpful with my daughter too. He was like a big kid himself, and she adored him. Not having much contact with her own father yet, she and James bonded quite quickly. A proposal of marriage was considered, but a few flaws started to show when it came time to deal with Avery about our children. James was jealous and acted extremely immature about the circumstances. He was only nineteen, for God's sake. What did he know of marriage, children, exes, and custody? Nothing! Except that I was his property now carrying his child. Wonderful. It turned out he was another possessive organism fueled with all kinds of testosterone that he channeled into control and domination—everything I was used to.

From Newman to Avery to James, it had always been about control. The power to have me do and think and live as they saw fit. How did such a free spirit end up caged behind the bars of male insecurity? I knew better than to be treated as such. But I had already broken the one promise I'd made to myself: that if I ever got married and had children, there would be no divorce. I did not want my children to grow up in a broken home. Yet we were broken—me most of all. Maybe this time I could keep it together. With a child on the way, two little ones, and one failed marriage, I would have to try harder. Be better. Give in more. Compromise. I had children that needed two parents. This would be my chance to prove to everyone that I was a good mother and took care of my kids. And just maybe, all those dried and splintered skeletons from my past would no longer poke through the ever-swinging closet door.

I was twenty-two and ready to burst with a baby. My C-section was scheduled for the very last day of March. Our new FHA home, which we were able to finance with a cheap mortgage payment, was also ready and waiting to welcome us all. It was on the same street I had walked a million times as a teenager on my way to meet friends, go party, or just hang out around town. It sat on a corner lot behind a gas station. I had never paid it much attention when I was younger. Shrouded in pines and vines, and all closed up, it had never looked all that inviting. But now the yard had been cleared, and the soft green grass and mulberry tree were unobstructed. It was two stories with a Michigan basement, which is all concrete, good for nothing but a laundry room. The living room was oblong and roomy with a nice kitchen that led to a stairway and second floor.

It was an older home, but clean and like new to us. With three bedrooms and one bath, it was inviting enough to make us proud. We welcomed our new baby girl home to her now two-year-old sister and four-year-old brother. I have to say, I was genuinely happy at that moment. I had all my babies together. She was pudgy and weighed exactly what her older brother had when he was born. And even though her dad had Maxwell House eyes, she stole my indigo blues. I was mesmerized and in love once again.

The weather blossomed into a beautiful spring, perfect warm thunderstorms and everything starting to bud. Life was as tranquil as an aquarium full of colored fish. Starting over wasn't as bad as I had anticipated. That is, until the bills started rolling in. We began to feel the squeeze of having to live from paycheck to paycheck. The stress was mounting. In just a few short months, we were arguing over the struggle of trying to become adults.

James was starting to resent the fact that he was the only one supporting us. He complained of having to pay for "kids that aren't mine." His rants sounded like this (at a volume I'm positive the whole neighborhood could hear):

"You should get off your a—— and get a job. I'm the only one making any f——' money around here. Shouldn't you be getting child support or something? I'm not doing this all by myself."

We did need the extra money, but his attitude ticked me off. I had three little kids to take care of. What was I supposed to do with them while I worked? Granted, I only had my son part-time, but he would still need supervision when he was there. We couldn't afford a babysitter. The only solution was to go back to work and let my mother watch the kids. Neither she nor Newman worked. He had filed for disability after an injury on the job. They still had the small two-bedroom home we had lived in when I was younger. And it was only a couple of blocks away. I had my reservations, but I didn't know who else would sit with a newborn and a toddler for free. My mother was thrilled at the idea but not so much about having to come to my home so early in the morning. Eventually she won, and the kids were bundled and packed into the car every morning, headed for Grammy's.

My going back to work did not fix our problems the way I thought it would. Now we fought because nothing was getting done at home. We'd come home tired, and I'd be the one who still cooked, cleaned, and got the kids ready for bed. James would come home, eat, smoke a joint, and fall asleep in the chair. He was also starting to treat my two-year-old daughter like she was nothing more than a pain in his rear. He nit-picked and harped at her so often it made *me* cry. The more I yelled at him about it, the more he'd yell at her. My poor, sweet daughter, who barely knew right from wrong, was being mercilessly persecuted for being a child when the real child in the house was him. He threw better tantrums than any kid I knew. I'd never seen a grown person roll on the floor, screaming and swearing at the stub of a toe. We didn't need an alarm clock because the first thing out of his mouth in the morning was, "*M—f—*!" I never knew why, but he made sure everyone heard it.

His conduct was ridiculous. It was as if he were a child trapped in a man's body. Where had this behavior come from? I'd never seen a man act in such a way. He smoked pot, which did seem to have a calming effect, but when he blew, everybody knew it. Day after day, the never-ending cussing and fits over senseless things started depleting any sort of concern I had for him. I was caught in a rage-infested bond with a man whose mouth struck at us like a diamondback rattlesnake.

Between his outbursts and "f—— you" attitude, it was no surprise when he was fired from his job. Now things would start going to hell in a hand basket. I would be the breadwinner for a while, while he slept, smoked weed, and hung out with his cousins and friends. The immaturity level I was dealing with made me fully understand why I had turned down his marriage proposal. I tried to love and nurture the madness he carried within him, but it was no use. He would no more listen to me than would a dog on the trail of a dead carcass.

I went to work every day, came home, made dinner, gave baths, and got ready for the next early morning. I needed a break. Feeling decrepit, I needed something to escape his outlandish and irrational behavior. I needed a drink.

"Get the f—— out if you don't like it!" he'd shout.

"You f——' leave!" I would howl back.

"This is my house! Take your kids somewhere else."

That hurt. I knew any inkling of love between us was swiftly fading, but I was unprepared for his coarse words about my children. The cuts were deep, just as Avery's had been. They came rolling out with such hatefulness that several times I wasn't even sure what I'd done to initiate them. Words are powerful. They can slaughter a soul. After a while, a heart that wants to love and be loved goes hollow, and self-mutilation begins.

I carried a heavy heart for many years. I just learned to live with it and with the crazed moodiness from the father of my child, hoping and praying she had been born with my mellower disposition. I had a temper too, but it took a lot for me to express it. I hated confrontation. I wasn't good at arguing. It was only after a dispute that I'd come up with clever stuff I should've said. It didn't matter what I said or didn't say, though. James never seemed to care either way. He was always right. There were times he felt bad and would apologize and even cry. This was all part of the erratic conduct I had to contend with. Still, I stayed, hoping I could save him and us. How? I didn't know. I thought if I just kept trying to show him love, he'd get it one day. He'd get that all I wanted was a family for my kids. A normal, healthy set of parents who did the right things by their children so they'd grow up to be decent, useful, pleasant adults. They needed parents who loved and respected each other, who were quality examples of how people should treat one another when they're in love.

I didn't want my girls to end up in volatile relationships, and I wanted my son to value women and treat them with respect. I'm still not sure of the full impact James had on my children, but I certainly know how much, how deep, and exactly what had been transmitted to the daughter we had. The older she became, the more noticeable it was just how much it affected her.

Recap

Staying in a relationship for the kids turned out to be disastrous for me. I lost my self-worth, independence, self-esteem, and joy.

Verbal abuse is mistreatment. It's just as damaging as physical abuse, sometimes worse. I shot back with my lightening tongue too, but was it really worth it? There is so much more peace to be found in making different choices in life and people.

I will not leave you orphans;
I will come to you.
John 14:18 NKJV

The Lord is near to those who have a broken heart,
And saves such as have a contrite spirit.
Psalm 34:18 NKJV

Chapter Eight

OLD HABITS

In 1998 the kids were eight, six, and four. As I had mentioned earlier, James and I were quite young when we got together; he was nineteen, and I was twenty-one. We partied on weekends to relieve the stress of the week. We'd usually have friends over to play cards, drink beer, and smoke weed. When James finally turned twenty-one, we started hittin' the bars. I wouldn't say we overindulged—not yet. We worked all week, and time just wasn't available. Plus, we had three kids that had to go to school every day, and that kept us on a schedule. Even with all the stupid, idiotic, and illegal activities we engaged in, I was proud that I had my kids on some sort of a timetable. They ate breakfast, lunch, and dinner at the same time together every day. They rarely missed school, and we tried to do family functions on weekends as often as we could.

By this time, James was working steadily for a union company and making a decent paycheck. I was a cook for a year, then a server for a golf resort, and finally a construction laborer myself. We had bought two jet skis, which kept us, our friends, and all the kids busy when the weather was cooperative. Barbequing, drinking beer, and socializing became our summer routine.

I was completely ecstatic when a phone call came from Avery that he was moving back up north with our son. The happiness that filled my heart is indescribable. I would now have genuine time with my first-born angel. He could be with his sisters, which was very important to me. But most of all, I would have my son again, and that put some pieces back into my broken heart, which had been shattered since I drove away that late summer day.

Things between James and me were still turbulent. We basically lived together as roommates, had sex when needed, and fought when the opportunity presented itself. My aunt, the one I'd lived with and was very close to, once asked me how I put up with him every day. "I'd go crazy," she admitted. I didn't have an answer. I just shook my head and changed the subject.

It was wearing me down. But since Avery was back, we had made an agreement for our kids to spend one week with him and the next with me. They would be spared the ranting and raving—to a point, anyway. With James' job in the Detroit area, it gave us all a break, which we—well, I—desperately needed. However, the old monkey was about to jump on my back again, cling to me like saran wrap, and stay there throughout the rest of our next five crumbling years together.

A mutual friend of ours, whom we both attended school with, had started dealing drugs. To my surprise, he was a huge cocaine supplier. Straight off the farm, he seemed an unlikely source. But there he was, and there *it* was, all laid out in gritty little lines once again. I knew that James had tried it, but that was about it. I, on the other hand, was way too familiar with it, and it had been so long that I was actually excited to do it again. It would be the beginning of the worst last years for us.

I didn't mind doing some, but I didn't like getting so wired that I became paranoid and useless. I valued my sleep, and that's one thing you sacrifice if you overindulge. At first, it was a gram here or there. Still functional, I could handle that. I preferred to drink beer to keep a balance of sorts. The coke gave me energy, while the alcohol kept me relaxed. There were times I overdid it, though, and would end up in bed wanting to rip my pounding heart out of my chest. Dawn quickly approached on those occasions, and I could hear the birds start to chirp. Coming down, eyes wide open, anticipating the alarm to get the kids up for school, was the part I hated most. To this day, I still sleep with a pillow over my head to keep the sun and happily singing birds from disturbing my senses.

But I kept going. I just tried not to overdo it so much. The kids were usually in bed or gone, but sometimes they weren't, and we'd sneak in and out of the bedroom, making excuses for what we were doing in there all the time. I felt much better if we went out away from the house; I preferred the bar or a friend's home. I always felt guilty for having drugs in my home with my children and being high around them. For the most part, I stayed in control as much as I could, while line after line attacked my arteries.

I still made dinner; James and I rarely ate, but the kids had to. I still ran their baths and lay in bed with them reading the books they picked out. All the while, however, I was restless to get up and out of there so they would go to sleep and not see Mommy's pupils, as black as olives, or sense my uneasiness. I kept it well hidden from them. At least I'd like to think I did.

James, on the other hand, was not so subtle. He couldn't handle it the way I could. Maybe it was a part of my motherly instinct to stay at least partly sound, while he would get so messed up doing one line right after another that by two or three in the morning he would have all the shades down and be peering out from behind them. Paranoid that someone was watching us, he'd spend the late night and early morning hours like that. Sounds like fun, right? It wasn't. But that's how we spent our time together.

I must say, we had quite a diverse assortment of characters in and out along the way. Most were high school friends or associates. Some were older than us; some were younger; and some were just plain weird. James liked to share with everyone and embraced the mixture of individuals. I didn't mind either as long as they weren't infringing on my children's time and space.

For James cocaine acted as a stimulant but also reduced his bipolar blowups. His mother had told me once that he had been diagnosed with ADD at a young age, so coke was almost like Ritalin for him. It made him nice, calm, and easier to talk to. But when he crashed, the war in our household left bombs falling all around us.

We were knee deep into it after about six months, buying on a regular basis. Our grams became eight balls and eventually ounces. We were supposed to sell most of the drugs to make our money back. Of course, that rarely happened. If it didn't sell right away, James ended up doing all of it. Most times I participated; sometimes I didn't. It was getting old again—the hangovers, the sore nose. I had done so much this time around and in the past that I couldn't even use my right nostril. It was too painful.

My foolish experience inclined me to introduce the foil. I take full responsibility for my part in everything and everyone I influenced. This story isn't about me being the better one, the stable one, or the sensible one. It is about me doing improper things, and it's ultimately why this section is called "Karma"—my karma, the things *I* did to cause the karma to keep building. In no way am I trying to make myself out to be a victim with a halo over my head. I am straightforwardly trying to own every single thing I did that was undeniably immoral, dishonest, criminal, and unethical. I had to become very honest with myself in the months before starting to put this on paper. I prayed for forgiveness and still do. It didn't matter how much or how little I did. I was doing it. I was performing an illegal and harmful activity while my children were home. I could've been sent to prison. God was watching; He had to have been. The only other explanation would be that I was a cat with nine lives.

Smoking cocaine off a foil is similar to smoking crack. I had not realized this until I quit doing it, unfortunately. It's so much worse on your body because you're inhaling chemicals from the aluminum, sabotaging your lungs, mouth, throat, heart and brain, as well as every other part of the body.

"Come hit this" was our constant refrain, and the tearing of foil went on and on. I watched James become more and more addicted. His desire grew so intense that he'd get down on all fours with a flashlight, searching the carpet for the minutest specks of rock he could find. It was so bad, his cousin nicknamed him Rocky.

He started missing holidays due to the aftermath of being up all night. He slept through two Christmas mornings, missing and ruining the joy that the day was supposed to hold for families. When I would try to wake him, he would just scream, "Leave me the f—— alone!"

This, of course, made me cry. I refused to use on that day. It just felt wrong. It always felt wrong, but I shrugged the feeling off every other day.

Christmas is supposed to be a day filled with love and families spending time with each other. It broke my heart that he chose not to be a part of it. He may have made it up for dinner, but then it was right back to bed. I was sickened that he could not exercise self-control, at least for his daughter's sake. I was ashamed of both of us and at a loss for an explanation to give the kids. It may have been the final stake in my heart. I'm not sure we were anything to him at all at that point. He was struggling, and my heart hurt for him. But my heart's bank of love and trust had been robbed for the last time. I stayed numb to him for the next couple of years before I decided I was done for good.

He had cheated on me by then, and I in turn did the same. Once my heart had been punctured by hurtful words and betrayal, the end was near. I had left and come back, left and come back, left and come back again, never quite knowing what was right. *Do I tear the family apart again or continue to be run ragged by his inadequate and sometimes terrorizing conduct?* During one of his crazed moods, we argued about me leaving. He took out a shotgun, laid it across the dresser, and refused to let me out the door. He was so fierce that he threw me on the bed. He held me down and bit my hand so hard he left a ring of teeth marks deep enough to draw blood, causing it to bruise and turn black, blue, and yellow. He was like some kind of rabid dog. I had bruises up and down my arms. A coworker took pictures because I was sure I'd end up with another

custody situation in due time and James would make the
same threats Avery had used.

Men always want to use the kids. That's where it hurts
the most, and they know it. My mother had also saved
recorded phone messages of James saying he would kill
me and everyone I worked with at the shop by blowing
us away with his gun. At that point, I had every reason to
believe him. But in the end, I went back, trying desperately
to keep us in the family home. I wasn't sure who had truly
lost it—him or me.

Recap

Drugs. What can I say? What a waste—a waste of time, money, energy, health, happiness, and your brain. They cause the breakdown of relationships, and the loss of time with your kids and family, and they can land you in the slammer. They're just not worth it.

If I could go back, I'd never try any of them. If you're having a problem with drugs or alcohol, I encourage you to get help.

recovery.org

Call 1-888-298-6689 to speak to an advisor.

Cast all your anxiety on Him
Because He cares for you.
1 Peter 5:7 NIV

Dear God, bring light to my day.

Raven

Chapter Nine

FLYING HIGH

By the year 2000, our home was in foreclosure. The drug bill was higher than we were, and no one was making the house payment. Two hundred and forty-two dollars and we couldn't manage it. How stupid. We ended up having to leave our family home and rent a two-bedroom trailer. It was snug for the five of us; but we all squeezed in, and nobody complained. I wasn't thrilled, but it was cheap and all I could find at the time.

The trailer had a large deck off the front, which appealed to me since I loved the outdoors and nature. It was surrounded by woods and had a beautiful creek down a small path from our yard. Secluded and quiet, it had trails running deep into the back part of the lot, which became my new course of contemplation. I enjoyed the isolation from all the traffic that had seemed to invade our house in town.

Still caught up in smoking through a toilet paper tube, I was informed that the factory I worked at was shutting its doors. I would receive TAA (Trade Adjustment Assistance) benefits and a one-time option for paid tuition to community college. This would also provide mileage reimbursement, job search assistance, and a relocation allowance. Going to college was something I'd always wanted to do, and this was my ticket. Even though I had dropped out of high school, the one thing I didn't mind Avery's mother pushing me to do was get my GED and my license.

The supplemental support from TAA was not very supportive, as it turned out. It was quite minimal. I would have to find another job. I took a position as a waitress at a local bar. James and I never hung out at that particular establishment. It was an old country bar that had been a brothel back in the forties and fifties. I was quite amazed and thrilled about the tips I was pulling in, though. I was able to help with most of the bills and buy food. James was working and helping some. Because of the cramped quarters, I was on a mission to find someplace a little bigger and better for us to live. Between my job and the supplemental income, I saved enough for a deposit on a larger home. It was several miles east of the bridge in my hometown, in another small town with a bar and a store. Still secluded, it was perfect and exactly what I was looking for.

A three-bedroom modular with two baths, a nice-sized living room, dining room, and kitchen, and only twenty-five dollars more than the rent for the trailer, it was perfect. The yard was large and open, and the river was just across the street down a two-track. I was in heaven. Being able to walk to the river was benefit enough for me.

By this time, James had lost three or four different jobs and complained of a back injury. His solution was to file for disability. He worked here and there, but most of his money went toward drugs. I had also found a new use for the little extra money I didn't have. It was the shiniest, tastiest morsel of any ill-begotten thing I'd ever laid my eyes on: crystal meth.

Methamphetamine, crank, ice, whatever street name you give it, I was instantly infatuated. I only knew of one person to get it from, so finding the glassy little tidbits was a sporadic event. But I had the connection and used every ounce of my female charm to get it. It didn't hurt that this person had had a thing for me since high school. He was a close friend that I took advantage of. Batting my eyes and flirting to the extreme, I always got what I wanted.

This infuriated James, but when it came down to it, he also used me as a pawn in the scheme to get more. "He'll answer your call," he'd insist. "He'll give it to you." During our now nine years together, James and I had tripped on mushrooms, eaten paper acid, and tried ecstasy in addition to the mounds of cocaine and weed. But this, this new stuff, was far more enticing and captivating than all those other drugs combined. It's hard to describe the bliss I felt while under its influence. First, it can be snorted, smoked, ingested, or injected. My nose simply could not handle any more abuse, especially since meth has an eye-popping-out-of-your-skull burn to it. It's no surprise I preferred to smoke it. "Chasing the dragon" became my new love interest. I got butterflies at the thought of seeing it, excited and giddy when I had it, and bummed when it was gone. The zenith of my favorite drug was sublime.

Just to clarify, I have never used a needle to inject anything. I hate needles and can't comprehend the thought of it—not that the way I did it makes it any less horrific. Meth gives you a long-lasting high with very little use. That's one thing I liked about it. Some people use a pipe, but true to form, a piece of foil folded in half was more to my liking. It gives you a high that doesn't turn you into a paranoid, high-strung, babbling idiot. You can stay very much in control on it. It keeps you alert and aware of your senses and surroundings. It makes you want to get up and go to work, clean the house, rake the yard, or party all night. Even with no sleep, you still feel competent and alive with energy, unless of course you stay awake for two or more days and your eyes start playing tricks on you. Then you start hearing things that don't exist and believing things that aren't true. I only experienced that a couple of times, but that was enough to warn me that it wasn't a good idea to go without food, sleep, or drink. In my use, I found a little goes a long way, and that was good enough for me.

Another highlight was that my use was virtually undetectable. No one could tell I was using. I talked right, walked right, looked okay, sometimes even better, and I could hide it. It was easy and allowed me to get things done without having to worry or jump out of my skin at the doorbell or phone ringing or when I came into contact with someone. It gave me confidence, stamina, and an erotic sense of sensual pleasure that helped emphasize the sexy self-image I tried to portray to the men around me.

I felt like a high-flying goddess and thought I looked like one too. These are the ways meth muddles your mind. You start to believe things about yourself and others that aren't true, to the point that you're convinced. I believed it heightened my perception. I felt psychic, thinking I could read thoughts and faces. I knew when to move, how to move, and how to maneuver people and their thoughts. It made me scheme and plot and figure out how to manipulate situations in my favor. I was in such an elevated state of mind, at times I thought I was some kind of tantalizing, mysterious temptress of the night who could perform powerful acts. I spun webs with my mind and caught flies.

Yes, I hid it well. Especially well hidden was my incessant need to pick. As seen on posters and commercials, the faces of meth users become riddled with scabs and sores from their digging at their skin. I was a picker, but not of my face. I was a scalper: I picked at my head where I had the cover of my hair to hide it. It would start when my head became tingly and numb and late at night when I was home or just bored. I'd use my fingernails to scrape my scalp until I felt what I thought was a miniscule bump. Then I would pick and dig at it until it bled and formed a scab. I would go to another spot while that one was drying up and do the same thing. I had about four or five spots like this. Once one was dried up and scabbed over, I'd pick all around it to lift the scab and pull it, usually full of blood, through my hair. For some reason, with that kind of high, peeling a scab was transfixing. It got so bad that my head would burn from shampoo, and the odor seeping from my scalp was rancid. I couldn't quite nail down the stench, other than that it must have been the combined scent of open flesh and the drug coming through my hair follicles. It was a disgusting thing to do, not to mention the possible embarrassment of someone noticing.

At the time, I was also studying and experimenting with witchcraft. I bought books and did online research, determined to become a solitary, ritual-practicing, spell-casting witch. Infatuated, I bought tarot cards and learned how to interpret them, doing readings for myself and a few close others. I believed in the magic and history of it all. I tried to become a moon-worshipping mystic.

Oh, but I knew better. I had been raised and taught that it was evil, the devil's work, black magic, a surefire way to hell. But I thought the flaming red carpet was rolled out for me anyway. With all the sins I'd been committing and the negative energy I'd sent out, I figured I already had one foot in the lake of fire.

The difference, I told myself, was that most practicing witches did not use their abilities for harm or foul. They were earth-loving spirits who used nature, herbs, the sun, and moon phases for healing and cast spells to ward off evil. There was a dark side—black magic, voodoo, and the occult—but I thought it just depended on what you intended to conjure. I certainly never wanted any part of the sinister side.

I'm naturally curious and love to learn, and I was very interested in that particular lifestyle at that particular time. I had no intention of becoming any sort of evildoer. It was a concept I found intriguing and still do. Only now, God has replaced my need to bewitch. As fascinating as I find it, among a lot of other things, my aspirations to become a witch have been laid to rest. I'm satisfied knowing I could be an "enchantress" or a different spiritual being devoted to God, His law, and His purpose for me.

Inside all this craziness, I had started college. James had received his disability back pay and had started building a house on some family property. I avoided him at every turn. My studies and my job at the bar kept me pretty busy, but I found myself spending more and more time at work. Indulging in beer and shots, I'd stay after my shift ended, socializing and having fun. This would be the beginning of my alcohol preoccupation.

Everyone knew about our on-again, off-again, convoluted, twisted relationship. James was never afraid to show his emotions in any form. If he was angry, sad, excited, whatever, he displayed it to anyone, anywhere. So of course, my coworkers and some patrons got a taste of this more than once.

The bar was fast becoming my home away from home. I pushed and prodded for him to get that house done. I wanted him out. He was building it for all of us, and I knew that. I think he thought the money and the house would keep us together. But I was done. He had drained every ounce of everything I ever felt for him. I pleaded. I begged. I talked and cried, trying to get through to him how he needed to change. The drugs were ruining him— us—all while I was still using them myself.

I thought I was better because I had a job, was working toward a degree, and was paying all the bills. The reality was, I wasn't much better at all. I was a hypocrite, a double-dealer. I was deceptive and critical, lying to everyone about who I really was. I was doing all the same things; I just reacted differently. The fact that I wasn't throwing tantrums didn't make me a better parent, friend, daughter, or employee. He definitely had some issues, mental or otherwise, but so did I. I kept them buried, but exhibited my problems in other ways, like drowning myself in fifths of vodka. However good, upright, or blameless I thought I was, the whole town was about to get a preview of just how corrupt I was becoming.

Recap

Drugs result in trouble of all kinds. Meth has got to be one of the worst. I'm not sure of all the materials used, and I'm not sure I want to know.

The idea of ingesting a combination of chemicals from God knows where really is sickening. In this chapter I enhance it. I talk about how good it made me feel. What I don't say is how much I deteriorated from it. Weight loss, rotten breath and teeth, memory loss, and dehydration are just some of the effects it has.

I am positive it contributed to my having cancer somehow.

Again the toll-free number for help is 1-888-298-6689.

*Be careful, or your hearts will be weighed down with
dissipation, drunkenness and the anxieties of life, and
that day will close on you suddenly like a trap.*

Luke 21:34 Today's NIV

May Lord and Savior give you grace

Through this test that you must face.

Our greatest challenge can be a gift

The pain and suffering He will lift.

A silent prayer I'll say today

May peace and comfort come your way.

Amen

Raven

Chapter Ten

SUMMER OF TEARS

By mid-2003, James finally had his house ready enough to be lived in. I was elated and relieved. I can't even express the peace within that came with his leaving. But on the outside, he made life a living earthquake. Of course, then the custody game started. He tried to take me to court for full parental privileges, but I convinced him he'd never win. We worked out an agreement that he'd keep our daughter while I worked and I'd have her on my days off. It made sense until he started controlling even that, refusing to let me have her when I was supposed to, out of pure spite and malice. We fought and fought over it, making our daughter miserable in the process. At nine years old, she took on the responsibility of taking care of him due to the guilt he laid on her, saying how he couldn't live without her, which made her feel obligated to stay even when I pleaded that she be with me.

Most of her time got spent with him. I was so tired of the fighting and arguing I basically gave in—another source of guilt I have to live with. Without my supervision or help, my young, precious daughter had to deal with a father who had no control. I felt useless, aside from being a drug-addicted parent. I had given in to a man I feared was losing his mind. Even though he had severe issues, in his defense, he was a doting father. I knew he loved his child, but caring for her in his messed-up state of mind made me sick inside.

All through her preteen years and into her teens, what should've been priceless and cherished moments made her depressed and withdrawn, angry and moody. She never seemed happy about anything. He stressed her out to the point I had to take her to the doctor for stomach problems and depression. He still didn't get it, and she wouldn't give in either. She felt so responsible for him it was sickening, and I did nothing about it. She knew he was troubled. She had witnessed his outbursts and his bullying me. He even went so far as to use threats of suicide as a tool to get her to stay.

Now I felt like the one who had gone off the deep end. Not only was I foolish, but my baby girl was taking all the flack and repercussions for our breakup. I was beside myself. Alcohol drowned out the thought of it, and it took a lot. I was ashamed at what I had allowed to happen to her, to all of my children. His badgering went on and on. He left harassing phone calls and messages, showing up at my home at all hours. My answering machine would be full of profane statements: "You're a f—— whore. You're never gonna see your daughter again. Piece of s——. I can't believe what a slut you are." He was relentless, treating me like I was some kind of bed-hopping belle of the bedsheets.

All of this, and only having my two oldest children every other week, gave me too much time on my hands, and I began to drink more and more. I went to the bar as often as I could. I kept up with my college classes, but even that started to avalanche. That roller coaster was about to lose some nuts and bolts and become one hell of a scary ride. Little did I know how close to death I was about to come in a series of drunken stupors. It was like being a NASCAR driver with no brakes.

The things about to happen to me would cause most people to reevaluate and make some changes right then. But guess what? They just drove me deeper into alcoholism and drugs, exposing my downward spiral to everyone, with me not giving one damn about it.

What a mess I was making of my life. I was driving my poor children further and further away from me. I missed countless basketball and football games and award ceremonies. I even quit going to their parent-teacher conferences. I was terrible about field trips and only went on one with each of the girls and not one with my son. Who was I to think James was the unfit parent? No matter what his chemical imbalance or extracurricular activities, he was always home with his child.

All the anguish I had stuffed down from the time I was four until this point had become a bubbling pot of poison rising to the surface because of everything I had been feeding it. I didn't want it to stop. Staying dazed and numb seemed like the only way to cope with the deep and somber hole I was burrowing myself in. The emptiness in my soul was too deep to fill. But I kept trying—and failing miserably—by accessing the only tools I knew how to use and becoming more hollowed out as each disastrous predicament came along.

St. Patrick's Day 2003. I had started celebrating at about noon. By this time in my life, a fifth of vodka was nothing to put down straight, no chaser. Blacking out became standard. I pounded liquor too hard to keep it from happening. By two thirty in the morning I hopped in my car, attempting to make the ten-mile drive home on my usually secluded, winding stretch of road. It was March, but it was still snowing, and the roads were slick, nothing unusual for northern Michigan. I deemed myself a pretty good drunk driver, even in winter. There is no such thing as a good drunk driver. Making the turn onto my road, I made it about a quarter mile, and that's all I remember. The car veered to the right and plummeted into the woods, taking down trees and a sign, eventually slamming into a large pine. I had passed out somewhere in the turn and awoke to the air bag with a face full of blood and a totaled car.

With a bloody nose and burns from the air bag, I looked as if I'd had a full head-on collision. Luckily, a man in a truck behind me saw it all and stopped to help. I sort of knew him. He was an older brother to a guy I went to school with. The shock of the crash brought me to my senses enough to know he would be a safe ride.

My mother, being a certified nurse's assistant, was the best option to run to so I could hide. I had to get out of there before the cops showed up and arrested me for drunk driving. It's no surprise my mom freaked out when she saw the condition of my face.

I explained, and she just shook her head, relieved it wasn't more serious but angry at my stupidity. It was not a pleasant scene. Between the ugly wounds on my face and all the explaining I had to do, the following weeks were full of advice.

"You better slow down, girl," a friend told me.

"Don't you know you could've been killed?" (That from my mother.)

"You better start taking it easy." (My boss's two cents.)

Yeah, yeah, yeah, I knew it. Now without a car, I'd definitely be slowing down since I would have to depend on other people for rides. But all that meant to me was that I could still get as trashed as I wanted and now I could put the burden of getting home on someone else. The audacity of my attitude was astonishing.

Feeling rejected by my kids and lonely, I just didn't care anymore. The guy I had been seeing was just using me for sex, when I'd thought I had seen so much potential for us. He never wanted me, just my performance. He was half the reason I was spending so much time in the bar. Wasting my time trying to convince him that I was good enough, I was persistent, but the longer it took, the more I drank. I was a hopeless, helpless, lost little girl. Though in my thirties, I was acting like a child. I was foolish and desperate.

Caught up in the thrill of the chase again, I was fixated on—even obsessed with—winning him over, so I just kept drinking. By summer I would be hit with yet another, more serious incident, more than driving into some trees. In fact, July 20 will forever be engraved in my heart and mind. Never had I witnessed anything so horrible and devastating. It put me in a place I had never been before and never want to be in again.

It was a Tuesday, one of those treasured Michigan summer days. The temperature was excessively warm, a perfect day for a river trip. Our trips consisted of any device that would float (I preferred a tube), a cooler full of cold drinks, and four to five hours of nothing but baking and buzzing in the sun. My girlfriend, her husband, and I decided to do just that. Coolers packed and canoe and tubes ready, we started out on our carefree cruise.

Full of sun, cocktails, and laughs, it was a flawless early afternoon. With temperatures in the eighties, the water had just the right nip. The river swirled us down, twisting and bending. Nature's critters romped and swam. Turtles, beavers, birds, and sometimes white-tailed deer, as well as mama ducks and their babies, were almost always visible. An afternoon like this was one of the most relaxing, pleasurable occasions in our small piece of paradise, a celebrated, almost sacred event.

A high in itself, nothing beats the fresh air, cool water, and warmth of the sun as the river gently rocks you leisurely along its winding path. That's how it starts out anyway. About halfway, the booze begins to merge with the heat, creating a sun-seared, brew-infused-brain, and the merriment begins. Loopy and laughing, Maria had a smile that was as white against her tan skin as the full moon in a midnight sky. She was an attractive woman. Of Native American and Hispanic descent, she had long, dark hair, and summer skin the color of Kahlua, accompanied by that stunning smile. Voluptuous, she carried herself as if she were an Egyptian queen. I often teased Maria, calling her Queen of the Nile while she sat upright in the back of their canoe. She was witty and charming, and she loved to flirt. Being from West Virginia, she gave us the gift of her sweet southern tone. She had no reservations about strutting her stuff. Whether we were on the river, at the beach, or at the mall, she was always polished and graceful.

She had married a guy I'd attended school with, and they had a six-year-old boy. Their marriage was faltering and sinking quickly. She had been having an affair with the longtime boyfriend of another one of my friends. I was in such a stupor most of the time, I hadn't even realized it was going on. By the time I found out and felt I needed to reveal the secret, the other friend already knew. Caught between the two friendships, I did the best I could to stay impartial. This was a small town after all, and having girlfriends worth keeping was a feat. I had learned long ago never to cross that boundary with a true friend. After breaking up a marriage at fifteen, I knew you just didn't sleep with another woman's man. I also knew, when told something in confidence, that's how you keep it. However, news of the affair was not told to me in confidence. Maria didn't tell me about it. James knew long before I did and let it slip. Let me tell you, she had balls to sleep with this woman's man. Pam was tough. You'd never know how threatening she could be because she was always jovial and smiling. She hit like a man, and every other girl was afraid of her. It was a crazy mixed-up situation. Everyone was losing their mind in one way or another. I never did hear of a confrontation between them. Pam and her man were done for anyway. Drugs had come between them, along with many other factors.

The day was winding down, and we were nearing a spot close to their home. Feeling pretty intoxicated, I couldn't judge their drunkenness. We had planned on doing a longer six-hour trip and had left their vehicle at the end to haul everything back. For reasons I don't remember, we decided to get off just across the road from their house. We'd been getting scorched for a good four and a half hours by then. My home was just a couple of miles down the road. Since we had no car, Maria's husband suggested we take his dune buggy to retrieve their van. Tipsy as I was, it sounded like a cool plan to me. The sun was still blistery warm, and a jaunt in an uncovered off-road machine might be rejuvenating.

All crammed in, with me in the middle of the two-seater, we started off, gravel flyin'. As I said, my house was about two miles from theirs, and the bar where the van was parked was probably another three. I had a thought that I might like to change my wet clothes before we got to the bar in case we went in for a drink.

Between the rumble of the engine and the wind howling in our faces, we couldn't hear each other unless we screamed. Hootin' and hollerin' all the way, we rounded the last curve before my house. I'm not sure how fast we were going, but it felt too swift for the curve we were trying to take. Just shy of my driveway, I motioned for him to turn in. That moment, the second it took for me to gesture with my arm, would change all of our lives forever.

The next thing I remember, short of the summersault I had just done, was standing up in my yard, disoriented. I looked over to see Maria's husband getting to his feet and the buggy overturned next to him. We both stood there a moment, heads spinning, trying to make out what had just happened.

That's when we saw her, Maria, lying facedown near the ditch. We ran over to her, falling to our knees, calling her name and waiting for a response. Any second now she would come to. Any second now she would wake up from the concussion that had knocked her out. Any second now … That's when I heard him scream, "Call 911!" and, with a heartrending sob, "I just killed my wife."

Half dazed and in shock, I ran for the phone. I must have called three times while waiting. The ambulance was about twelve miles away. The whole time I kept waiting for her to pop up and ask what had happened. With my knees shaking and my hands trembling, I looked down and saw the one thing that would haunt me the most. Her blood had pooled on the grass by her head, and a piece of brain tissue lay next to her ear. Her head had been severely fractured by the buggy flipping over on top of her.

I fell into a dizzying, grim blackness. Somehow I had managed to call my mother, and I remember her helping me into the house as the police secured the scene. Through a blur of tears, all I could see was the white blanket they had laid on top of her. *This can't be real. Any second now, I'll wake up.* A shrill of fear filled my insides as I thought about their boy. He was only six. What kind of explanation do you give a young child for his mother not being there to tuck him in that night? Or for that matter, the rest of his life?

For about three days, all I could do was stare into space. The dismal reality of seeing my friend lying dead in my yard stayed cemented in my brain for months. Not wanting to be alone, I stayed with my mother for a few days and even with James for a week. I slept with the lights on for weeks when I finally could return home and manage to stay there. She was gone. Really, truly gone. It was heartbreaking, and I was not equipped to deal with such a tragedy.

Every morning and night from that day forward consisted of trying to fall asleep with the image in my mind of her body on my lawn covered in a white sheet. Morning coffee was at least a couple-hour daze lost in reliving the events from beginning to end. No matter where I went or what I did for at least the next six months, some piece of that day stole any concentration I tried to hold. I kept trying to find a way to make that Tuesday different in my head. It was no use. Whenever six o'clock came or the sun would blaze on a weekday or the smell of the river drifted along on the summer air, every detail would replay, and I had no button to shut it off.

My only saving grace was when my kids were home. But without them, I'd turn to liquid torture until my memory obeyed and went black. The cold weather began to toboggan down from Canada, and suddenly there was a welcoming snow. Summer was over and with it the dreadful vividness of those dreary recollections. They started to fade, just like the sun when the winter season approached. Despite all the times I had sought God in my desperation or imagined a message attached to my failing, not once do I remember thinking of Him during this time.

Once again, another piece of my unsettled and distressed emotional heart was locked away in the denial pit. I couldn't face it head on. I didn't know how. It was like watching myself go through the motions without any attachment to my feelings. Yes, I was sad and terribly empathetic toward her son, husband, and family. But otherwise I stuffed it away, put it behind me, and tried to act as if it hadn't happened, at least not the way I saw it.

If only I hadn't motioned for him to make that turn. If only I hadn't been so selfish, wanting to change my clothes because I was worried about going into the bar. I blamed myself, and I didn't know how to face that either.

I descended even deeper into my liquid world, trying to drown out that day and the guilt I was carrying. I found my favorite drug and took myself up, up, and away from all thoughts of it. My life was in shambles. I ended up dropping out of college for the simple reason that now I had an excuse. Sure, I wanted a degree and to actually finish something for once in my life. But rather than focus on any goals or accomplishments, I just took another way out, sealing myself up in a tomb of toxins, the way I had done for years. I told myself to forget about the past, the hurt, the memories, and even the good things. They were gone, and there was no sense in reliving any of it. I kept covering it all up with made-up perceptions and phony emotions, knowing that if I compressed it enough, it would stay down deep, though it would play havoc trying to float to the top. When clarity is the last thing on your mind, the strongest part of you will keep everything crammed in the belly until eventually the dirty, awful nasties need to be regurgitated in order for you to get well.

But I wasn't ready to get well yet. In fact, things would begin to mudslide once again down a slippery slope of thick, heavy uncertainty. I wondered if this time would be it. I was almost positive I'd reached the underbelly of it all. I had just witnessed death and had a near-death experience myself, but now I would face the long arm of the law.

Who had I become? What was I doing? The drugs had distorted any sense of finding the right direction. One thing I've learned: you can't escape being unaccountable forever when there is a balance due.

Recap

We all know the devastation drinking and driving causes. So why do it? Getting caught can cost bundles of money these days, time in jail, and the loss of your license, your pride, and possibly even a life.

My experiences in this chapter should not be taken lightly. Although it still took time for me to learn my lesson, the point for you is to get it now! And try to help someone in need who is battling the bottle.

Weeping may stay for the night, but
Rejoicing comes in the morning.
Psalm 30:5 Today's NIV

Far locked away
were thoughts of that day
The rippling water, the laughs and the sun
A day made better by good friends and fun
Late afternoon, skin warming and tight
Fun time was over, a friend losing light
A turn and a tumble, a life on the ground
Cries and then silence when finally we're found
It's not true, it's not true, it can't be this way
How could this happen? What do I say?
I'm sorry forever that you were the one
I'll join you one day when my journey's done

Raven

Chapter Eleven

SCARED TO DEATH

We were approaching the one-year mark of the buggy accident. James and I were still haggling over custody. His abrasive persistence was getting old. He was still filling my machine with angry, nasty name-calling, and then begging and pleading to talk, and finally crying with threats of suicide.

We had just had an altercation and had to have a police officer come to his home because he was refusing to let me see our daughter. To make himself look like more of a fit parent, he told this particular officer that most nights he could find me weaving my way home from the bar down the long and curvy road I lived on, which was true. Anything he could use to ruin my days and nights, he most assuredly didn't miss pointing out. The officer agreed to let me take my daughter anyway. Thinking all was good and the officer could see through James's maniacal rants, I figured I had the upper hand.

I came to find out, exactly two weeks later, I had nothing of the sort. On my way home after closing the bar, I found myself being pulled over—by the same officer. I was too stupidly drunk to realize how drunk I actually was. But I remember thinking that I was gonna get away with it. *He'll either give me a ride or let me walk*, I thought. I knew this officer. He gave my friends breaks all the time. I imagined he wouldn't arrest me since our sons were also good friends.

He made me get out and perform the standard tests. Believe it or not, I failed my ABCs of all things. And that was it. Handcuffs were latched, and I was hauled to the station in the back of the cruiser for the first time in my life. I had been pulled over once and let go but never given a ticket.

I blew a .20, and the judge said no one should be on the road in that condition—another proud moment for my children. I swear I must have been in a coma for years. Not one thing that should've been considered hitting rock bottom had registered at all. I couldn't see how deeply I was hurting my kids, the harm I was doing to myself, just what a fool I was becoming, and how much I looked like one.

But my downward spiral continued. Being convicted of a DUI and spending one night in jail would not compare to what I would face next. How long before a person gets it? What really has to provoke someone to stop her in her tracks? Only the individual knows for sure, but it can take a long time to come to one's senses, if one ever does.

This is exactly what it means to be "saved by the grace of God." Time after time my life could've been over, by way of death through overdose or any number of vehicle or freak accidents. But this next incident would be a doozy. I still have a hard time believing it actually happened and that I blocked any sort of breakthrough or recognition at the seriousness of it. All I know is, my heart was in my throat, and I would be left on edge for months. It was just one more potentially fatal conclusion to yet another one of my reckless choices.

So far, in 2005, I had totaled my car, nearly killing myself while driving home drunk, gotten pulled over while heavily under the influence, gone to jail, lost my license, and had to move because I lived too far away from anyone to get rides. Since watching my friend depart from her mortal existence the year before, work had become a burden as well. I was lost, absent from my own existence.

A week before the Fourth of July, some friends and I were celebrating early. The local bar I frequented had a slightly seedy reputation for drug use and distribution by patrons as well as employees.

The four of us were taking pleasure in using some cocaine that one of them had scored that day. With parking behind the bar, access out the back door to the car was easy. Parking was in the alley, not seen from the main road, and the only thing behind the alley was the Catholic church. It was the perfect cover from prying eyes that might have an interest in the suspicious activity we were engaging in. Of course, we all piled into the car at the same time because that meant more lines for everyone if each of us doled out a little of our own stash.

We weren't long into our festivities—in fact, it wasn't even dark yet—when we made our third or fourth trip out to the car. We were all talking and joking, just starting to loosen up, when all of a sudden a deep voice out of nowhere shouted, "Get your hands up!"

I looked up from the baggie of white substance I was holding to see guns pointed at the car from every direction. In a split second, I put my hand with the baggie down next to my right leg and dropped the bag onto the floor. I was hoping that, by not having it on me, I wouldn't get into any trouble.

Just then the doors flew open. The guns were still pointed at us, and more orders were shouted. "Everybody get out and keep your hands up!" Holy crap, this was an actual SWAT team bust. The four of us peons, who'd never had a serious drug charge, were being held up by STING (Strike Team Investigative Narcotics Group). It was so surreal and unlikely it was almost comical. But trust me, I was not laughing. When there's a group of gun-toting investigators in your face, you don't make light of the situation.

Unbelievable! Once again, there I was in a bad state of affairs. *How does this keep happening?* I asked myself. I figured I was probably going to jail for a long time. Even if I didn't have the drugs on me, they were near all of my stuff, and a pack of cigarettes that had a straw in it was stuffed in my purse. When told to grab any personal belongings, I stood still and took nothing. Wise? I'm not sure, but it was worth a try.

I didn't know how long I'd be locked up, but it would probably be extensive. Possession of cocaine is a serious charge. I was too high at the time to fully comprehend the gravity of the daunting weight that would surely pull me into the depths of hell. *I can't go to prison. What about my kids? What are people going to think about me now?* It was a whole lot to ponder, and I did not want to think of the worst-case scenarios.

Much to our surprise, no one got arrested that night. Although, they had found all the drugs and a bag of pot, it all had to be sent to the lab for testing. So, like any other brain-dead zombies under the influence, we carried on to the house of the "supplier," and our party ensued, our pupils dilating as we talked until the wee hours of the morning about the alarming uncertainty of our fates.

How does a thirty-three-year-old mother of three with an already poor parenting track record find the dignity to put one foot in front of the other after such asinine activities? How does she hold up her shame-filled face through all this humiliating disgrace? There was no way around this one. I had degraded my family to the lowest degree. They had had enough, and frankly, so had I. But it was too late. It was time to pay the piper.

After meeting with my lawyer, I discovered I was facing a minimum of four years and a maximum of *twenty*. Now, that was scary. I'd kept thinking I was untouchable— *invincible*—that maybe I was being protected by some spell I had conjured previously. But deep down I knew a day would come, and I'd have to pay with my life. It was only a matter of time before something like this happened. I had gone on too long on the devil's playground, and now I was caught in his snare.

Still, in the very deepest depths of my despair, I held out hope. I hoped that by some twist of fate it would go away, that somehow I wouldn't be held accountable enough to spend years in prison. However daunting the thought, I was prepared to do my time simply because I knew I had it coming. I wasn't a dealer. I wasn't even close to being a part of something that would call for SWAT to raid me. If anything, any of the years before with my exes would've substantiated an arrest. But those days were over. I had become a recreational user and purchased very little—and even those occasions were few and far between. Still, I had been there and a willing participant. As scared as I was, I was willing to stand in the truth.

In a lucky sort of way, I had been temporarily disconnected from the cocaine and meth by circumstances out of my control. A lot of busts were going on, sending everyone into a panic. Yet here I was facing time in prison for one stupid night of pathetic gratification. The next couple of months were nerve wracking and intense, to say the least. Every time the phone rang or a car door shut, I'd jump higher than Michael Jordan with a basketball. *This is it—they're coming for me.*

The waiting was torture, and I deserved every bit of it. I had played and won for far too long. The levy was going to break sooner or later. The news of my fate came through an unlikely source around the end of August. I was working a day shift at the bar when my boss, of all people, nonchalantly spilled the beans. "By the way, I heard you're not being charged with anything."

I shook my head as if I'd heard him wrong. "What did you just say?"

Still looking down at his paper, he spoke quietly. "I can't say who, but someone I know at the courthouse told me you're not in any trouble."

My stomach fluttered and flip-flopped. "Are you sure?" I could hardly contain myself.

"That's what I heard, but you didn't hear it from me."

My heart was pounding. My head felt like it was on spin cycle. Unbelievable! No charges? No court? No going to prison? I wasn't sure if I could or should believe it. But I trusted him. Why would he lie? It was one of the most unusual and miraculous turns of events I'd ever been involved in.

Not one phone call or visit from a police officer or agent. Not one word from the court or my lawyer even. In fact, that was the last I heard of any of it concerning me. None of the other three were charged either. How did that happen? Most of the time in the drug world you get out of trouble by "rolling over" on someone; you give up the name of someone else, a bigger fish, in exchange for a lesser charge or immunity from prosecution altogether. Some people thought that's what I had done. I really didn't care. I knew I hadn't. I was free, and that was all that mattered.

I had prayed for God not to take me away from my children, though I was least deserving to even ask. However, the most loving, generous, caring Creator honored my wishes, and I never understood why. I should've been burned at the stake so many times over, but there He was each and every time, protecting and shielding me from all the harm and destruction I had invited into my life. I had let my turmoil carelessly infect the lives of my children. How miserably sad and embarrassing it must have been for them to be attached to a mother who had less than cared for them and their feelings, who took every selfish step she could find to bruise and batter their childhood memories, who allowed their friends, friend's parents, family, and school faculty to look at them in pity and shame. I still pay a price with the looks I get from certain people in passing.

It has gotten easier the more I talk to God and learn to forgive myself. And sometimes in the deepest, darkest part of the night, when it's just me and my thoughts, silent tears fall from my face, reminding me just how lucky I am to have a forgiving God who loves unconditionally. I'm also grateful He made my children in that very same image. I would be lost without all of them.

Little by little, pebble to stone, I started building a straighter path out of the rocky terrain and darkness, trying to scrape up the tiny shards that were left of my self-respect, self-worth, self-esteem, and pride. I had been lackadaisical for the past six years, and I was slowly starting to see the bigger picture.

One of my attributes is the ability to bounce back from anything, dirty face and all. I've somehow always found a way to stand and march headfirst out of the murky muck I've submerged myself in. Proud? No. But you can't bury your head in gunk forever. Life has to move on. Nothing ever happens overnight for me. So the tiny pebbles and stones I had started to use to get my footing took an abundance of time before they turned to yellow bricks so I could find my way home. The vehicle of life that had been cruising in the fast lane was slowing. The blinker was on, and I was ready to change lanes and slow down. I still had a lead foot, but I was learning to obey the speed limit.

Recap

More drugs! If I haven't said it enough, I'll say it again: they are not worth it. Life is so much better with a clear head. You really can enjoy it without them. I'm living proof of that.

Instead of using, I now write, read, surf the net, draw, take walks, play with the dog, visit family, crochet—whatever it takes to keep my mind healthy and occupied.

Having a terminal illness is a benefit. Yes, I said *benefit*. It ensures I won't use unless I want to rush my way out of here. I want to live—and not behind bars or hooked to a bunch of tubes in a hospital.

Please think twice before getting involved with drugs. There is no good that can come from it.

This is the verdict: Light has come into the world, but men loved darkness instead of light because their deeds were evil. Everyone who does evil hates the light, and will not come into the light for fear that his deeds will be exposed. But whoever lives by the truth comes into the light, so that it may be seen plainly that what he has done has been done through God.

John 3:19–21 NIV

Chapter Twelve

AN ANGEL APPEARED

The years 2004 and 2005 were tough. Losing my good friend in front of my eyes sent me tail-spinning into a world of brainlessness for the next year. By 2006 the internal storm had calmed enough for me to see through the rain and stand upright in the wind. There was certainly no pot of gold, but there was perhaps a hint of a rainbow.

Bar work was becoming less desirable. I wanted weekends off to be home with the kids, and I didn't want to work weeknights either. It suddenly hit me: *Hey, you do have some college courses under your belt, enough to warrant applying for a desk job of some sort.* And that's exactly what I began to do. I typed up a resume and began sending them out to every available opening I could find. In the meantime, I quit the bar to spend some time with the kids. My oldest was driving by then, and when that happens, seeing them is rare. But we made the best of it, and it felt good to be at home. I did go out occasionally when they were having their "dad time." But I slowed down considerably.

A couple of months went by, and I started to worry I might have to go back to waitressing. Money was getting tight, and just as I was about to make a phone call to my prior boss, the phone rang. I was asked to come in for an interview the following morning for a secretarial position. I was so ecstatic I looked like Tom Cruise on Oprah's couch. The kids were equally excited. I followed up with a second interview and landed the job.

It was July 20, 2006—exactly two years, to the day, after the accident that had killed Maria. I thanked her, and my new morning shift was born. The downside? A shrilling six o'clock alarm in the mornings. Not being a morning person, I'm not pleasant at that time of day and never have been. Bar work does not consist of early mornings, and that was all I was used to. I've always been a night owl, preferring nightlife to any sunrise socializing. Needless to say, the first month or two was turbulent. But I gradually formed a practice of the acceptable kind and settled in to learn and do my best. My job required etiquette, not bar behavior. I had a lot to learn.

I still went out, overdoing it at times and then stumbling in to work half drunk and hung over. It took some getting used to for all of us. Luckily, I knew the family well, and they were generous enough to let me slide more than a few times. I wasn't quite sure what to do with myself in this new, composed arrangement. Less drama. Less worry. Less trouble. No one jumping out of the dark. No freak accidents and less misfortune.

While my work situation was showing promise, my love life was limp. I was in limbo, sad to be alone, and longing for the gentle and soothing touch of a man's arms embracing me. I missed the feel of family—Mom, Dad, kids—and it was almost Christmas. Melancholy started depositing pieces of gloom.

I was doing my best to properly conduct myself in the workplace, hoping to rebuild my unfavorable reputation and be the mother my children needed. Like I said, it didn't happen overnight. Then I had a bright idea: maybe James and I could give it one more shot. I was lonely. He was lonely and still crazy. I'm not sure which one of us was more unbalanced.

My poor daughter had spent enough time with him by now that she became his caretaker instead of the other way around. It was breaking my heart to see her carry such a heavy burden. I felt I should intervene and take some of the pressure off her. I thought that might put everyone at ease by pulling us all back together. The fact that I ever came up with that harebrained idea only highlighted my unpredictability.

I knew James in and out, so there were no surprises, nothing I didn't expect or couldn't handle. The selfish part of me wanted someone to hold me again. I knew he still loved me and would take all of us back in a heartbeat. This was another thing I never understood about the men I'd been involved with. No matter how awfully they thought of me or treated me, they always wanted me back. If I was so revolting, why in the name of Pink Floyd would you ever want me back? It made me believe deep down that I was worth having at least.

I wondered amid all the changes if maybe now he and I could function together. After all, he could be very tender and caring when he wanted to be. Without the drugs and alcohol, he was pleasant, other than his normal frenzied temper over nothing. *So, what the hell?* A nice new home that was built for me and the kids? I had to give it one more shot.

By spring of 2007 we packed it all up again and headed for another round in the ring. I thought I was doing the right thing for my daughter. Even as young as she was, she was wise, and I should have heeded her warning. It turned out to be a disaster. It started out fine, until we jumped right back into what I describe as graveyard love. By that I mean the drugs, the drinking, the arguing, and digging the same six-foot hole that we'd been buried in so many times before.

I can't even tell you my state of mind. I had no idea what I was doing, trying to save us all from the dysfunction and mayhem, all the while creating the most we'd ever been in. I became more mentally unstable and lost than ever, losing myself in bottles of vodka and baggies of meth, pulling all-nighters with friends, and never explaining where I'd been or why. It was a foul thing to do to anyone, even James. Even viler, my children witnessed most of it. The karma just kept building. I was an inconsiderate person. But the whole time, I didn't see a damn thing wrong—not with me, anyway. It was short and sweet. After one year, it was over … for good. No really, for good this time.

I couldn't keep inflicting grief on him, on me, or on the kids. That much I knew. Just after the first of the year, I rented a very lavish house on the river from my employers. They kindly made the rent affordable. I leased a brand-new Jeep Commander from the boss's daughter and returned to the bar on weekends for extra money. I was trying to start a new phase, hoping my new engagements would trigger bigger changes.

Unfortunately, my drug use and drinking were still wreaking havoc, but slowly I began to take a small bit of pride in myself. I started to see just how fortunate I was to be able to enjoy life on the river in a secluded, expensive home, to drive one of the best vehicles I could ever afford, and to have two jobs to help me stay out of trouble. I was looking for a break in the clouds.

In mid-January 2008, while getting ready for work, I noticed a lump in the middle of my throat. During a routine visit to my gynecologist, he noticed the bulge and recommended I have it checked out. Another saving grace, it wasn't serious or cancerous, just a growth on my thyroid, which was removed with an easy outpatient operation. I healed within days with no meds. I'd thought for sure I had cancer then. For whatever reason, God had pardoned me once more, even if I still hadn't accepted him yet. He sure was being good to me. Why? I had no idea.

In the midst of my trying to be a better everything, He did another incredible thing for me. He sent me an angel. While I was at work at the bar on a cold and snow-stuffed night in early February, my eyes fell on the man I would spend the rest of my life with.

I turned around from grabbing a bottle of liquor only to see a bubblehead—my name for a snowmobiler. He was dressed in a colorful combination of riding gear: a green and black Arctic Cat coat, an orange Harley-Davidson sweatshirt, and bright yellow gloves. I would later tease him about it. He approached a bar stool, staring me down. "You're back," he said, with a gaudy smile.

We had met a couple years before when my head was stuck in fifths of vodka. My memory of that time was hazy, but I recalled him to be pleasant and courteous. I smiled back, unsure of how to react since I couldn't quite call to mind all we had actually shared back then. I knew we had slept together, but I had been so wasted I couldn't revive the experience. So I just played it off, changing the subject and trying not to look like an idiot. My shift ended shortly after he arrived; so of course I sat down next to him, and we drank and talked until closing.

He gave me one compliment I had never heard in all my life: "I like your vein." The left side of my face has a prominent streak of blue right down my cheek. He noticed. I was dizzily thrilled. We spent that night together, and I knew without either of us saying it that we were destined to be a team. The more time I spent with him, the more my heart settled into the possibility of making him mine for good.

I had finally found someone to love me for me. No yelling or screaming, he was the exact opposite of everyone I had ever been with: quiet, sensitive, soft spoken, sincere, and sexy. I loved everything about him so far. He sweetly took his time with me. God had sent someone impeccable, a guardian angel I most certainly believed I didn't deserve but whom I needed as much as the air I breathed. He made me feel that I was worthy of having good things in life. And he wanted to give them to me—*me*—the girl who lived her life on the edge, doing all the wrong things while trying to find value in herself, the one whose exes told her she was a stupid b——, a useless whore, a piece of s——. He saw me as a soft, delicate flower, someone who needed to be handled with care. He brought out the loving and silly side of me, the girl who only ever wanted to be loved as much as she wanted to give love. My true smile was restored.

Allen and I were together every weekend after that until we were married a year later. He gave up his house in the city to move north where we would live in his cabin. Only seven miles from the town I grew up in, his cabin had three bedrooms. Perfect for me and my girls. My son had graduated by this time, but all the kids took to him. My youngest held off a little longer, but eventually her heart would find a place for him too.

We embraced each other and our life together. God had shown His mercy once again by sending one of his angels to watch over me. I felt special in his presence. Always the center of attention, I was high on him alone.

I inhaled his kindheartedness, and for the first couple of years we were ablaze in passion and bliss. But old habits come alive like vampires in the night, and our happy union would start to crawl its way into the mausoleum of matrimony—which is how this story begins.

God asked me specifically why I would forsake the man and the wonderful life he had brought to me. I, in my soul searching, dove deep into the heart of my pain, clearing the cobwebs from my conscience and my subconscious to discover the real truth of why I wanted to walk away.

I was getting older. The gypsy in me bought a brand-new pair of running shoes. Fear of commitment and being tied down led to my leaving. I was a free spirit. What business did I have being married again and allowing another man to tell me how things were gonna go? Not me, Mister. I am well of age to control my own life and decisions. But the thing was, I'd never done a good job at it before, and this time would be no different.

I wasn't used to staying in one spot. I had made twenty-six different moves in my life. I was always unsettled, never unpacking. It was too comfortable with Allen, safe, dependable—all the things I never had and wasn't used to. I thought I knew what I wanted, and I knew those things were good. But in my mind, I wasn't good enough for them.

I was a vodka-slammin', cig-smokin', drug-token, man-eating, hello–good-bye kind of girl. Deep down I knew it was what I needed, but the person I was and the life I knew wouldn't allow me that much acceptability. I figured Allen would end up giving me a one-way ticket sooner or later anyway. I might as well hop the first train outta town before he got the chance. The money was saved, and in a few months, I would've been off to New Orleans. But my new life would begin right here. God said, "You're not going anywhere." And He meant it!

Cancer *had* to be my last wake-up call. They say it will kill me eventually. I would've ended up dead sooner, had I not called Allen that day. I'd rather ascend to heaven with the peace and serenity I have found through this disease and knowing true love from the grace of God and His mercy than live through the cataclysm I'd imposed on my previous being.

A diagnosis of terminal cancer demands that you examine every aspect of your life. There is no other choice—at least there wasn't for me. Being told you might die within a few years makes it mandatory to reflect and consider all the consequences of your actions, past, present, and future. Without my facing all the raw dynamics, my spiritual growth and health would have remained hindered.

Through it all, I would learn to forgive myself and love myself and others in order to let God's plan manifest in me. Cancer was God's final attempt at getting me to take notice. I was forced to find the layer of attentiveness under all the sticky pride, embarrassment, and shame and take a long, hard look at my children. But once I did, once

I could see and think clearly, I became intensely aware of how exquisite, smart, beautiful, and loving each of them is. I could finally see all the wonderful qualities I had been cold-shouldering and missing.

And oh, the guilt and remorse that came fizzing and burning like chronic heartburn after I'd chipped away at all those emotional truths. But it was a must for my healing, emotional and physical. I found secure and steady ground where there's light, love, joy, and peace. I have found felicity in my surroundings.

Recap

Slight changes can make a difference. A pebble will grow into a stone and then, eventually, into the rock that will hold you in place. Sometimes we can't give up everything all at once. But making subtle changes helps. Take a job that requires more hours. Serve at a soup kitchen. Meet people who do not use and invite them to have lunch or coffee or ice cream. Take a ride. Go to a park with the dog or kids.

Little things can lead to bigger, better things too. Remind yourself how awful you felt the last time. That was a huge help for me. Pray. Find a church to attend. God will help no matter what your situation. You just have to believe He will.

Truly the light is sweet and a pleasant thing
It is good for the eyes to behold the sun.
Ecclesiastes 11:7 NJKV

Good Morning
Burning candles light the way,
Prayer and mantras start my day.
God and angels keep me on track,
Spirit and nature give what I lack.
Family and friends love to the core,
My wings are lifted, from cancer I soar.

Raven

Chapter Thirteen

KARMA POSITIVE

After my diagnosis, the initial shock, the pain, the surgery, and finally the physical healing, the authentic recovery began. The honesty of every single part of my past began to emerge. I began to add up the collection of fate I had brought upon myself, and it became clear exactly why I was in the position I was in at that moment. As agonizing as it was, I sat in throbbing anguish, crying and torturing myself for every last mistake I could recall. I begged God for life and forgiveness, every day asking Him to hold me up and make me a better person.

I needed—I was dying for—redemption. A ton of clutter obscured my soul. The ugly energy I had put out into the world, along with all the senseless grief I had caused people I loved, was sitting in my intestines. A bulk of thick, scuzzy smut had piled up in my stomach in the form of a tumor, needing amputation.

Mistakes, bad judgments, and bad decisions: I had lied, used, abused, and manipulated my way through the hearts of many, not giving a second thought to how those hearts would endure the misery I had inflicted, not only onto them, but onto myself as well. I was selfish, thoughtless, self-centered, and greedy. If I could go back, I'd kick my own a—, all the while asking, "Why would you do that?" The bigger question is, why didn't someone else kick my a——? Maybe God knew I never intended anyone sorrow, knowing the suffering I had gone through myself. My carefree attitude got me where I am today, wondering when I'm going to die from a cancer for which there is no cure.

The long road from wasted to deliverance, from booze to the Bible, has been worth the battle I fight now. There is no one sin greater than another. I may as well have committed them all. My life was a circus, from silly to repulsive, from offensive to beautiful. I have emerged from the decaying cavity that was my life with many blessings. I thank God every day for them.

I'm especially grateful for my three delightful children, whom I can't get enough of. I sometimes wish they would burst through the door at four o'clock from the school bus just so I can have that time back, that time to make them dinner, help with homework, read them stories, and tuck them in with kisses and hugs. Don't ever take your children for granted. They grow up and then they leave. They become their own people with their own lives, and then *they* get to decide how much time you get with them.

Cancer has united us even though I neglected the time I should've given them. I know my moments with them are precious. We say "I love you" often, and the hugs are plentiful. Of course, I could never get through life without my angel of a husband, Allen. He loved me more than I loved myself at a time when I needed it most. He never gave up on me, even when he had every right to. I truly believe he is part of God's plan for me.

I was ready, prediagnosis, to fashion a new life without him. God stepped in with one last attempt to make me do the right thing. I'm positive that, if I hadn't called Allen the day I woke up with cramps, I would've been dead within a month or two. When God relays a message of this magnitude, there is no denying it. Every one of my senses was opened in compliance. I prayed and I pleaded and I listened. At last He had gotten through. His message was received and well taken. The girl I'd been, the girl who had gone through life as a wrecking ball, died the day she got serious about prayer.

I began praying every day, still unsure of what I was supposed to do next. The people on my forgiveness list were quite long, but I started asking. Journaling became essential to my daily routine, helping to get my feelings out and on paper. I needed them staring back at me to put denial in its place. The more I talked to God, the better I felt. I started thinking about possibilities and opportunities and how I could become of service to Him. The answer came, and without delay, I honored His calling.

I got going on reading books and doing research online and decided to write the book I'd been carrying inside me for years. I prayed for His words to fill my mind and heart and move my pen. I asked for the book to become a message from Him to share in hopes of making a difference in someone's life.

How we live life is a direct result of the amount of peace, love, and joy we experience. Our intention in everything we do will find a way back to us. It may take a while to reap the benefits, but if our intentions are positive and we are well meaning, we will be blessed.

My story has been one filled with cause and effect. If God hadn't allowed me to cross so many boundaries, I would have no reason to follow Him now. It's so easy to get caught up in worldly pursuits, especially if you're the only believer among your friends and family. Most of my friends are still out partying, and I don't see them often. The inquiries have stopped for the most part, and visits are even less frequent. I don't mind. I am happy right where I am, doing what I should've been doing twenty-three years ago.

There are temptations everywhere. I am reminded every day of my faith. Having a terminal illness and a colostomy bag ensure that I won't venture too far from the place it took me so long to get to. They remind me of the past I've left behind and of how the present is a gift. I have to be thankful for that. It is God's way of saying, "You've had enough fun. Your playtime is over. It's time to be responsible and well." I had many chances to get a clue, and I chose not to every time.

Every action has a reaction, and these days I practice making my intention and energy positive in all I do. "The wages of sin is death" (Romans 6:23 NKJV), no matter how big or small a wrong it is. I have learned to take in the smallest of miracles in this world. My awareness and appreciation for the little things have been heightened. I watch the sun's golden glow on the trees as it sets, and say, "Thank you." I watch the birds and squirrels at my feeder a little longer. I listen to the wind as autumn comes rolling in, and again I say, "Thank you."

Soon winter will clench her frosty teeth into our small northern town; sometimes when she comes, she doesn't let go until June. I look forward to the holidays as I get to have all my children home. No occasion is taken for granted when you're not sure if you'll see the next one. God will keep me here as long as I'm needed, until all my lessons have been absorbed and hopefully shared by this story.

Sometimes sitting in your pain causes all the tears needed to replenish the lake, the lake of people's hearts that you pumped dry by being selfish, insensitive, uncaring, and unloving. Sitting in clarity when your mind isn't clouded and shrouded in the cover of addiction can be overwhelming. But it is the only way to find peace and heal. Forgiving yourself becomes tangible, and the pain subsides. I found my way to that place through prayer.

It is evident that I was drowning in a cesspool of detriment, and He saved me countless times, showing me that I do have purpose and that I am worthy to be loved in the right ways. If you're sitting in darkness, I would like to help you find the light through Jesus Christ. No matter what you've done or what you're facing, the Bible says that "whoever calls on the name of the Lord shall be saved" (Romans 10:13 NKJV).

This simple but beautiful scripture is one I use for a prayer:

> *Cause me to hear thy loving kindness in the*
> *morning, for in You do I trust.*
> *Cause me to know the way wherein I should*
> *walk, for I lift up my soul to You.*
> (Psalm 143:8 NKJV)

I have included some other lovely prayers in the back of this book. One of them is a prayer to accept the Lord as your personal Savior. I have to say too that the Bible is an essential book to have. I never realized the many lovely and comforting writings the precious book holds. The book of John is said to be a helpful start upon first reading. My daughter gave me one of those small Gideon

Bibles that kids get from Vacation Bible School, and I started by opening it randomly, hoping there would be a message just for me that day. Even if I didn't understand what I read, I'd pray the Lord would open my heart and mind to its meaning. I love the introduction in my tiny Bible. It states: "Read it to be wise, believe it to be safe, and practice it to be holy. It contains light to direct you, food to support you and comfort to cheer you. It should fill the memory, rule the heart and guide the feet." And that's exactly what it's for and what it does.

There are quite a few Bible translations that use language that is easily understood, for example, the Common English Bible, the New American Standard, and the New Living Translation, to name a few. The Internet is helpful for finding one that will fit your style and be the easiest for you to understand.

If you do not have a Bible, prayer is always something you can do that is free and at your disposal. Prayers can be as simple or elaborate as you want. "Thank you" is a great invocation. Only you know your heart and what you need to say. Just say it. God hears all requests, big or small. He invites all conversation too. That's what He's there for, and so much more. I recommend *Illuminata* by Marianne Williamson. She writes such wonderful devotions. Try writing your own.

Listening for God's answers used to be difficult for me. Now I use silence and my intuition to help guide me. Sometimes His messages come by way of dreams, verses in the Bible, television, conversations with friends, nature, or many other ways if you are willing to pay attention. God loves all people and rejoices when even one finds courage to accept His presence and everlasting love in his or her life. Our earthly time is short, but with Him, we can make it so much more joyful. Having cancer and including God in my life has made it the best it's ever been.

The lyrics to Tim McGraw's "Live Like You Were Dying" are so true. You do talk more sweetly and love more deeply. I have to love and give freely with kindness and compassion to all. It is one of God's lessons for me. I coined the phrase "keep kind in mind" as a reminder to love and give as God would.

My daughter's psychology book, *The Science of Psychology* by Laura A. King, states, "Writing about your deepest thoughts and feelings concerning your most traumatic life events leads to a number of health and well-being benefits." Experiences in nature have been said to have the same effect.

Nature has been a staple in my steps to endure my life with cancer; just a few moments outside to breathe fresh air, listen to the birds, watch the squirrels, or take a peek at the moon and the stars does wonders for me. A simple walk around the yard can be therapeutic. Fresh air is the breath of God.

Cancer doesn't have to be a dead-end road. It's all in how much you want to live the kind of life you wish to create and in finding joy in the time you have. Sadly, we often don't welcome grateful and necessary changes until a traumatic event comes along, and the earth below us begins to tremble, knocking us on our buttocks.

Every life lesson prepared me to weather this one dark endeavor. I've been through more valleys than peaks. I had to refocus, shifting my view from being sick and dying to being useful, active, and alive. And so can you!

Let your roots grow down into Him and draw up
nourishment, so you will grow in faith,
Strong and vigorous in the truth you were taught.

Colossians 2:7 NIV

I appreciate seeing my breath in the cold,
reminding me that there are many
more treasured breaths to take.

Raven

Thank you, God!

Appendix

Courage

Having courage means conquering fear or despair.

In life there are many things that require bravery. This can be a huge feat for anyone but especially for a person with a terminal illness. Some days you don't even want to get out of bed. Then those tormenting thoughts slither in, when all you think about is dying, and the emotions crush you. It is tough to remain content all the time. But faith and hope sprout courage.

It has taken fearlessness to admit on social media that I have a colostomy bag at forty- two and that I believe in Jesus Christ and the word of God. It has taken fearlessness to talk about my past mistakes and the hurt I've caused, to go out in public with a bag attached to my stomach afraid it will make noise or carry an odor. It has taken fearlessness to be intimate with my husband and to carry on with chemotherapy appointments when all I want to do is stay inside and sleep. It has taken fearlessness to face mortality, to smile in the face of uncertainty, to admit I was an alcoholic and drug abuser, to admit to my affairs, to go after my dream of writing a book, to ask for forgiveness, to admit being molested, to tell the truth, to be brought back from the dead exterior where I had barely existed, and to teach of God's love, letting people know He can change their lives.

Because of the defects in four adult males, I now have the nerve to stand up for myself. Verbal abuse gave me guts to speak up and endurance to do what must be done. I'm not afraid to wear pajamas anymore, because the scared little girl I was doesn't have to worry about running in the middle of the night.

I no longer live out of boxes. I've allowed myself to unpack because the uncertainty of when I might have to leave has gone extinct. I am home, never to make the twenty-seventh move—ever. God has prepared a place for me on earth, and I look toward Him as he prepares a home for me in heaven.

I had to rise from the bottom of shame, depression, and denial, using my daring spirit to help me back up. I was destined to be where I am now, trying to get a message out with my new living voice. It was God's plan for everything to happen just as it did. My tenacity came from Him.

The ultimate test of fearlessness is facing God's will. Although I believe in miracles and my faith is strong, I am completely aware that my time may be limited. I have never revealed to anyone the truth of how I feel deep down about my illness. And that is this: God is giving me time to serve His purpose and right my wrongs. Only He knows how long He has allotted for that. But honestly, I don't think I'll be here as long as I would like. Of course, that's up to Him. Maybe I'll do so well on my lessons, He'll exonerate me from my tribulations and prevent what my doctor says is inescapable.

The days continue to roll over quickly, and I thank Him when I wake up for another tour of duty on His planet. Even now, as I near the end of my prose, my body has started to change. My last MRI showed a new tumor on my ovary. My targeted therapy had run out of steam, causing a mass to form. Now I have to switch to a pill form of treatment and one of the last regimens available to me. But I know God has something planned for me, even if I run out of medication.

I was diagnosed within months of three other people. Two were family members. My maternal grandmother was also lost to colon cancer two years before my diagnosis. The three have all passed on, leaving me to wonder when my expiration date will be. No one wants to think about dying. It hurts to think about all the years I wasted worrying about what kind of buzz I could catch next. Even worse is knowing I was so emphatically careless that now my nights are numbered.

I try not to think of it as punishment, but we all know what goes around comes around. Karma and cancer give me the courage to face it, and God gives me the strength to shoulder the negative karma, incurable cancer, and courage I need to deal with all of it.

I still struggle with the fact that I will never be that pretty, young-looking woman I once was. My skin is dry and cracked. My breath has the odor of sickness. I have gained thirty pounds and have cut off my wavy locks due to chemo evaporating their moisture.

And how could I forget the colostrophe (my word for colostomy)? Next to making amends with God, that has been one of the biggest changes needed in my life. How so, you ask? I made a deal with myself. I could have had it reversed, but I knew exactly what would have happened if I had proceeded with that. Without it I'd be off and running, using cancer to condone getting into many of the worldly cravings that had brought me down in the first place, feeling sorry for myself and allowing self-pity to justify the things I'd choose to do. So I decided it was not in my best interest to be that free. I needed a tether of some sort. What better than a bag of poo hanging from your side?

Cancer wouldn't be enough, and I think God knew that. I've always needed boundaries. Unfortunately, when I did have them, I hopped the fence anyway. This time I would not allow myself to take the easy way out. Too much is at stake. I need to be an example for my children, even if they are adults. I need to do the work God has set up for me and do my best to be a good and giving person. Having discipline and being held back from the desires that get stirred up in me, such as wanting a strong vodka and Mountain Dew (or ten), or seeing an old friend who still looks cute all dressed up and knowing that will never be me again—the confidence, the flirting, being keyed up to grab the attention of anyone at any time—has all been a part of the reason a noose needed to be put on my life.

I do have those nights when I just want to fall back into that old skin and go play like I was a single, childless woman. The urge to drink away my troubles and smoke my fears absent with a meth foil does cross my mind. That is when prayer steps in again and keeps me grounded. Talking to God talks me out of slipping back into the past. I strive to stay on the right path. There can't be any going back. Another request I offer up to God is "Please don't let me lose my mind and forget everything you've given me to think about, see, and learn."

I scare myself at the thought of being given a "deadline." Six months? A year? That's when things could go haywire. It will be a huge test of my faith if that day ever comes—unless of course, I'm too sick and it won't even matter. But I get the feeling that's not how it's going to go. God will probably be testing me right up to my deathbed. He knows me inside and out and knows I need protection from striking the match of desire.

Writing, reading, and learning are my drugs of choice now. God has issued me different ways to use my tools for the good. One gadget has stayed the same … the pen. I no longer search frantically for the classic white Bic Stic pen so I can pull it apart and use the stem to smoke meth or cocaine. I tore apart countless numbers of those infamous white pens with the blue caps. Everybody had them. They were much sturdier and safer than plastic straws, which often caught on fire and melted almost up to your lip. Toilet paper tubes were simply too big for meth foils.

For many years I did this and never gave a second thought to the discourtesy I was showing such a beneficial instrument. This came to me one day while writing in my journal and thinking about how much I love to write longhand instead of electronically. There's just something about the way it feels and looks. It's something valuable from your very own hand.

It hit me what a natural high I had just putting ink on paper—the same kind of bliss I encountered while using drugs. But now I'm happy, comforted in fact, and so peaceful that it's my go-to for placidity.

How ironic that I have taken the same apparatus that used to give me pleasure and the risk of death and turned it into joy by using it the correct way, the way God intended. I went from "How soon can I get a drink or a hit?" to "How soon can I get to my desk and write?" To feel that pen flow across paper is the best, cleanest high a person could hope for.

The audacity to take on cancer is the biggest test I've ever encountered. I think I'm passing that test, and

I hope to be an inspiration to others struggling with tiny battleships sinking around them. But we have to continue building for ourselves the ark that will save us from the downpour of bad news, sickness, anxiety, and just plain fear, giving us safety against the flood of the internal storm-driven sea that is cancer, drug use, or abuse. Our relationship with God can be the ark. In the midst of the disheartening feelings we cannot help from invading our imaginations, He'll help to keep us afloat when it feels like we are sinking from ill-fated news.

Like newborn fawns with wobbly legs, we eventually learn to get up and walk confidently into battle. Even if we have lost the mother doe, our strength with God makes it possible for us to master any negative experience. Keeping a resilient spirit and optimism, not only for ourselves but for our loved ones, saves us from falling victim to a monster that can be combated with God's grace and the safety of His arms. What a wonderful feeling that all we have to do is ask.

There will be those days of helplessness and hopelessness. Let those feelings emerge. The tears, the fear, the anxiety—let it flow, and then let it go. It's cleansing, and once it's over, it's over. Move on and start to appreciate what you have in this very moment. It will allow you to start living your highest purpose. Search inside for whatever it is that brings you joy and a sense of pride. Use those tools to build brighter days full of the light that God intended for you to shine with all along.

Wherever you are in dealing with the cancer journey, drug addiction, or pain from past events, you can still make a difference. Try doing something you once loved. Do something for others. Send a comforting e-mail, say a prayer, or call someone and tell the person how grateful you are to have him or her in your life. Little things can transform someone's day as well as yours. The Bible is also a good place to start. Besides teaching us how to live in the likeness of Jesus, it offers within its pages comfort, peace, and so much wisdom to feed and breathe life into our souls. My life may end due to cancer, but I am thriving because of it. God mercifully guided me back to where I needed to be. Home. His hands are a chrysalis for my existence.

A cheerful heart is good medicine,
but a crushed Spirit dries the bones.
Proverbs 17:22 NIV

Normal

Back to normal will never be,
My search I have found a kindlier me.
Forgiveness and love now lead the way,
Opened my eyes the price I must pay.
Can never go back and that's all right,
Darkness is gone gave way to the light.
Thanks to God for giving His grace,
The past is a dream I no longer chase
New life, new me, my soul is free.

Raven

Colostomy Information

A colostomy is defined as "a surgical operation in which a piece of the colon is diverted to an artificial opening in the abdominal wall so as to bypass a damaged part of the colon (or large intestine). It leads to no control over the passage of stool from the stoma" (the end piece that sticks out of the belly).

I can't tell you how many times I've finished a nice clean shower only to hop out and get halfway dried off, when all of a sudden my stoma decides it wants to be amusing and literally shoots stuff all over the place, down my leg, my foot, the floor, and splatters all over the wall and toilet. Then it's time for shower number two. That's enough to dampen your day (pun intended). It's not so bad if it cascades down my leg in the shower, but of course that usually never happens.

I have always been a private person when it comes to anything involving the bowels. I never found humor in passing gas, neither the smell nor the sound, or in how big the excrement in the toilet was. For some reason, my family gets a kick out of that stuff.

God certainly knew what He was doing by using colon cancer to get my attention. Out of all the body parts He could've chosen for me to deal with, it had to be something involved with the entrails. My business is done hands on every day.

It was so horrible at first. The chemo made it very loose and sloppy. And the smell would gag a maggot. My husband's grimace told me how bad it was. I wasn't sure I'd ever get to the point of handling it without thinking, *I hate this*. But after two years, I've come to accept what will not change and have found ways of taking care of this rosy-red poop chute.

Now that I've been switched to the pill form of chemotherapy, the whole formation has changed. The texture is harder and less soupy, and the odor is not quite so offensive. It no longer makes my husband's nose crinkle. It is definitely easier for cleaning purposes and changing gear. The odor is now at the level of baby poop. Cleaning takes less time, and fewer bags are needed. It's still unpleasant and my least favorite thing to do, but I've learned to live with it by telling myself it could be worse. It really could be.

Now that you are aware of my feelings on the matter, I have some tips to offer up for anyone searching for what to do and what not to do. These are my own personal opinions, so please do not ignore your doctor's orders if you were given a certain set of instructions.

I posted this information on my blog, and let me tell ya, it took a good long tennis match in my head to finally decide to do it. Nobody wants to hear or talk about it really. If you're like me, you either try to figure it out on your own, or you search until you find what you're looking for instead of asking.

In the two years I have been "fecally challenged," I have come to learn a few tricks that may help make life a little easier in caring for the somewhat convenient poop dispenser:

> First of all, baby wipes or moist towelettes are an absolute necessity. I started out with damp paper towels. Yuck!

> When I begin my shower, if I don't have to change the flange, wafer, base, or whatever you call it, I remove the bag and clean the stoma area as best I can with the wipes. Once in the shower, I let the water rinse off any loose bits. I keep a few wipes in the shower at all times to wipe the area after it's wet and for when I get out.

> When done in the shower, I use the wipes to cover the stoma before wrapping a towel around me, so I have no worries about soiling the towel. The wipes cling well until you are done drying off (let a couple dry out beforehand).

> Before snapping on a new bag, I use baby powder to help dry the area and defend against odor. It also helps later when I need to change the flange.

> If I am changing the base or the flange (they last about three to five days) with the bag off, I use the adhesive remover pads to dampen the tape against my skin. I rub the damp remover wipes over the top of the tape, which helps to loosen it. Then I grab a loose piece of the tape and proceed to wipe around and under it, until all the tape has been loosened from my skin.

> ➢ With the inner ring still attached, I get in the hot shower and let the water and soap help loosen the rest. Once I'm done washing my body, I use my washcloth with one hand and direct water from the shower to pull the wafer off. I soak the cloth and squeeze under the ring until I am able to pull it off completely. I always keep the garbage next to the shower to throw in all pieces of yuck before, during, and after my shower.

> ➢ Once the flange is off, I use a generous amount of body wash, cheap shampoo, soap, and baby oil if needed to scrub the remnants of adhesive left from the tape. Dial soap works best for removing the stickies that are left when pulling the flange off. When all is clean and I'm all done, I put a wipe over the stoma (they work better if dry) before putting the towel around me.

> ➢ Bathing isn't too bad. I usually keep one of the drainable pouches on, or take everything off completely, as long as I'm sure my bowels are on a break.

The stoma paste, I have found, is just a waste and makes a bigger mess. As long as you keep the area clean every time you change the bag or flange, there shouldn't be any problems. But this is just my personal take on the matter. I also do not use the skin barrier wipes that supposedly help with irritation. They do not work for me. I simply use a minute amount of baby powder around the sticky part of the skin—but just a tiny bit, otherwise the tape from the base/wafer will not stick. Even if it's a little loose in some spots, as long as the middle part that is cut to fit remains secure, that's what matters. Also, a little baby oil in the bag against the stoma helps everything slide and makes for less bulging.

The baby wipes are also handy for cleaning the ends of drainable pouches. Using air freshener before and after changing bags is helpful if opening a window isn't feasible for long periods of time, like during the winter in northern areas or in motels that don't have fans. In addition to air freshener, lighting candles or blowing out matches can help with odor in the bathroom. Of course, fresh air is always best along with an exhaust fan.

I make sure I have everything I need ready before I get in the shower: a cut flange, a bag, baby wipes in and out of the shower, a wastebasket, a towel, baby oil, and bleach. Bleach comes in handy if any accidents should occur. I find the spray kind, such as Clorox Cleanup, is easier.

These things should also be included in a travel bag. Instead of a wastebasket, bring extra garbage bags (bathroom size), some type of deodorizing spray, and extras of everything.

Let each of you look out not only for his own interests,

But also for the interests of others.

Philippians 2:4 NKJV

Be eclectic, eccentric, and electric!

Prayer

Prayer is a lifeline straight to God. *Merriam-Webster's Dictionary* defines it as "an earnest request or wish" and "the act or practice of praying to God or a god."

Matthew 6:9–13 NKJV contains the Lord's Prayer. The scripture says, "In this manner therefore pray: Our Father in heaven, hallowed be Your name. Your kingdom come. Your will be done on earth as it is in heaven. Give us this day our daily bread. And forgive us our debts, as we forgive our debtors. And do not lead us into temptation, but deliver us from the evil one. For Yours is the kingdom and the power and the glory forever. Amen."

It was taught to me as a young child. I have never forgotten it. When you don't know what to say, this is the prayer to use. I am a tremendous believer in prayer; you might call me a prayer enthusiast. To me it is the most sacred act between a person and God. You are communicating directly with Him. There is no fonder joy than speaking your most sincere words of gratitude to the being who made you.

Faith in Him is hard to have. I completely understand that. Why believe in something you're not even sure exists? But why not accept it? I would rather die believing and get nothing in return, than die a disbeliever and find out there is something truly wonderful waiting for us on the other side. What have you got to lose by having confidence that your spirit will live on forever in a heavenly place?

Of course, it takes a little more than that. You also have to believe that Jesus walked this earth and died on the cross for us. He was a human just like you and me, but He was the Son of God. He followed the Word and did everything God had planned out for Him, even death. Why would He do that if there wasn't a reason? He could have failed and been just like the rest of us walking around lost today. But He believed, had faith that God would keep His word, and He would ascend into heaven with the angels after being crucified.

The Bible says in John 5:24 NKJV, "Most assuredly I say to you, he who hears My word and believes in Him who sent Me has everlasting life, and shall not come into judgment, but has passed from death into life." That means if we affirm that Jesus is the Son of God and follow His word, we will live forever in a kingdom of wonder and beauty after we pass on. I don't know about you, but that's where I would like to be when my time on this planet is done.

You can't get to heaven just by being a good person. There are a lot of good people in the world, but the Bible says to have faith and He will return someday. Revelation 1:7 NKJV states, "Behold, He is coming with clouds and every eye will see Him, even they who pierced Him. And all the tribes of the earth will mourn because of Him."

It's difficult to deny the words of the Bible, with so many testimonies of Christ by the men who saw and wrote about Jesus, and all the amazing stories they told. I mean, who would think up those kinds of things and write them down if they were not true? The Bible is an incredible manual full of inspiration, hope, good will, and nourishment. I was fascinated by some of the scripture I was reading after my old life slid off like a popsicle in summer. I had not picked up a Bible since I was twelve years old. As an adult, I came to see what joy, love, and peace the text contained. I could go on and on about the Bible, but what I truly find phenomenal is prayer. It gives me such comfort and peace. And not only that, God answers prayers. Sometimes it is on His time and not ours. We have to be patient. Prayer just feels sacred, especially when I look outside and see the trees, birds, squirrels, and everything that was created by God. Sit with that a moment. *Every living thing was created by God.* There is no grasping the awe of it.

When I pray, I feel better, lighter, like a weight has been lifted from my body. But even better than that is praying for other people. Even the words "thank you" are a prayer. It's so easy to pray. I have written several that I'll share here and have also included some by others, which I hope will help you and give you a sense of peace.

Prayers by Raven and Others

Dear Lord, may Your hands and all health-
care professionals' hands become one
Intervene in the scientific world, dear
Lord, that a cure may be found
Show your mercy on all who suffer
from cancer's invasion
Lift our spirits above pain and sorrow
Thank you, dear Jesus

Amen

Raven

Lord, walk with me every day
May I be healed, not lose my way
Help my feet to stay on track
Put strength in me that I may lack
Lord, take the pain and give me peace
Help the fear to be released
This I ask of you, my Lord
I pray my body be restored

Amen

Raven

May you hear the birds sing in the morn
With faith be lifted from the storm
May Jesus take from you your pain
No more worries and peace you'll gain
Be made new in days to come
This I pray, His will be done

Amen

Raven

Lord, I am blessed and I thank you for that

Free from my bondage and frostbitten path

My bones were dry and water was far

You carried me miles, erasing my scars

Your grace, it has saved me time after time

My battle within an uphill climb

Now I am safe in your loving arms

Free from the fear and life full of harm

Amen

Raven

Dear Lord, thank you for giving me

Parents/grandparents who loved me

As their own, may their spirits from

heaven be angels that surround me

Amen

Raven

Another day Lord is all I can ask

So undeserving because of my past

But you're so forgiving, amazed by your love

Comfort and hold me as if I were your dove

You're gentle and meek and mild; all things

As soft as a whisper or angel who sings

Just one more day, Lord, I ask in your name

To finish your work and give back the same

Amen

Raven

To Receive Christ as Your Savior

Confessing to God that I am a sinner, and
believing that the Lord Jesus Christ
Died for my sins on the cross and was raised for my
Justification, I do now receive and confess
Him as my personal Savior.

Amen
Gideon Bible

The morning blushes with pink surprise

To a world with hollow eyes

Oh, nation of death, can't you see the dread?

Invite the peace of our Supreme God

Stop the madness and violence abroad

Turn back to prayer, reject the hate

Save your souls, clean your slate

The King will come, he'll reappear

Mercy of Christ you need have near

Bow down and pray like never before

Hate, prejudice, greed, and war

Together let's stand and close the door

Raven

Glory be to the Father

and to the Son

and to the Holy Spirit.

As it was in the beginning is now,

and ever shall be,

world without end.

Amen

worldprayers.org

Life is short and we have not too much time
for gladdening the hearts of those
who are traveling the dark way with us.
Oh, be swift to love! Make haste to be kind.

Henri-Frédéric Amiel (1885)

worldprayers.org

Prayer is not asking.

Prayer is putting oneself in the hands of God,

at his disposition,

and listening to his voice in the depths of our hearts.

Mother Teresa

To everything there is a season,

a time for every purpose under heaven.

A time to be born and a time to die;

a time to plant and a time to pluck

up that which is planted;

a time to kill and a time to heal …

a time to break down and a time to build up;

a time to weep and a time to laugh;

a time to mourn and a time to dance …

a time to cast away stones and a time

to gather stones together;

a time to embrace and a time to

refrain from embracing;

a time to get and a time to lose;

a time to keep and a time to cast away

a time to rend and a time to sew

a time to keep silence and a time to speak;

a time to love and a time to hate;

a time for war and a time for peace.

Ecclesiastes 3:1–8 KJV

The Lord is my shepherd; I shall not want.

He makes me to lie down in green pastures;

he leads me beside the still waters.

He restores my soul: He leads me in the

paths of righteousness for His name's sake.

Yea, though I walk through the valley of the

shadow of death; I will fear no evil for You are with me;

Your rod and Your staff they

comfort me.

You prepare a table before me in the

presence of my enemies: You anoint

my head with oil; my cup runs over.

Surely goodness and mercy shall follow me all

the days of my life; and I will dwell in the

house of the Lord forever.

Psalm 23, a psalm of David NKJV

Recommended Reading

- The Bible
- *One Heartbeat Away*, Mark Cahill
- *Light the Flame*, Andrew Harvey
- *The Book of Awakening*, Mark Nepo
- *Peace from Broken Pieces*, Iyanla Vanzant
- *Illuminata*, Marianne Williamson

Websites for Prayer and Inspiration

- biblestudytools.com
- guideposts.org
- joycemeyer.org
- learntopray.org
- worldprayers.org